THE CIVIL GRACES PROJECT

The Pursuit for Common Ground

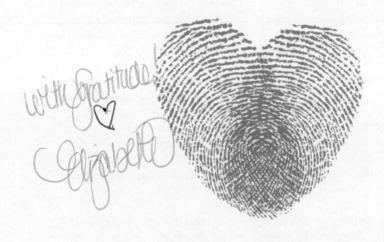

With gratitude! ♡ Elizabeth

Elizabeth Moro

BALBOA.PRESS
A DIVISION OF HAY HOUSE

Balboa Press books may be ordered through booksellers or by contacting:

Balboa Press
A Division of Hay House
1663 Liberty Drive
Bloomington, IN 47403
www.balboapress.com
1 (877) 407-4847

Printed in the United States of America.

ISBN: 978-1-9822-5059-1 (sc)
ISBN: 978-1-9822-5061-4 (hc)
ISBN: 978-1-9822-5060-7 (e)

Library of Congress Control Number: 2020912962

Balboa Press rev. date: 08/18/2020

Out beyond ideas of wrongdoing and rightdoing,
there is a field. I'll meet you there.
When the soul lies down in that grass,
the world is too full to talk about.
Ideas, language, even the phrase "each other"
doesn't make any sense.
The breeze at dawn has secrets to tell you.
Don't go back to sleep.
You must ask for what you really want.
Don't go back to sleep.
People are going back and forth across the doorsill
where the two worlds touch.
The door is round and open.
Don't go back to sleep.

—Rumi

I do not fear...It was for this that I was born.

—Joan of Arc

Dedicated to my dad—the one who taught me to dance through it all.

CONTENTS

PREFACE

From my earliest days, I remember loving two things: the political process and dancing. One might say one part needed the other to make it work! My favorite dancing partner was someone who I knew loved to dance as well. He had my mom twirling around the dance floor when I was a twinkle in her eye, and theirs was a love like Fred and Ginger. They gracefully glided around the space in perfect step with each other—unison.

With our big Midwestern family, weddings and celebrations were a regular occasion. I would be out there with my cousins cutting up the rug, but I always saved a dance for my dad. He intuitively knew how to lead, and even with my impetuousness, I would gracefully fall into step. I would trip on his toes, and he would chuckle and say, "That's okay, sis. Do you want to lead?" Laughing, I would acquiesce because I knew better than to try to outshine a pro.

I was born the day after President Harry S. Truman died. I still have the note with the scribble: "Baby Girl, 11:11 a.m. Pres. Truman died." For as long as I can remember, before leaving to do anything, my dad would call out after me, "Give 'em hell, Harry!" which was a popular slogan from the Truman days. This book is my attempt to reckon my dance with the steps taken to do just that.

Just before Christmas 2015, I lost my dancing partner. His heart gave way, and he got his wings. My life would never be the same. He sent me another someone to keep watch over me, and I still miss those big blue eyes that would let me know everything is going to be all right. I miss those massive, mitt-sized hands that would brush away the tears.

He and I had a common bond. We loved to watch political conventions after he finished his long days in his radiator repair shop. I told him someday I would be the first woman president. I've always been a big dreamer and was passionate about honoring the suffragists whose sacrifices allowed me to be on the ballot in the first place. My grandmother was an elected official, and I always felt the desire to serve was in my blood. Maybe it was the eight brothers, but fighting for human rights came naturally for me. After my race for the U.S. Congress a few years ago, I wanted so badly to talk to him, to apologize that I didn't make it. I promised him that I would someday run like Kennedy and make a better world. It crushed me, and the world felt like it was falling in on top of my heart.

In the years that have passed, in subtle ways, my dad has summoned me back on the dance floor to bring the world into harmony and a whole new dance. It was an invitation to open my heart to welcome people who were afraid of showing up. It was a call to share our universal truths and to carry on a message of love that the world so desperately needs. It was a call to remember what makes life so extraordinary, especially in a country so richly blessed and richly challenged as ours.

I created the Civil Graces Project as much to understand my own existence as to help others find the reasons for theirs. It seeks to open us to the paradoxes and life-changing moments, to ask, “What is the meaning behind all this?” and to see the changes in our nation and question whether we have lost our way.

Despite all the shake-ups and letdowns life has presented, I’m still a dreamer for a world where we can make things equal, free, happy, and more loving for everyone. Part of that began with loving and forgiving myself for not always reaching the ideals I held. There must be peace within if you want to create it around you. Like my dad would say, “If we can’t make peace in this house, how can we expect to have in the world?”

Here’s to creating peace in our world, and to our angels who pull for us on the other side.

WHAT IS THE CIVIL GRACES PROJECT?

> A nation born in revolution will forever struggle against chaos ... Our story isn't over. It is up to us to write the next chapters.
>
> —Jill Lepore

You are invited to embark on a journey that has the power to transform your life and the world around you—the Civil Graces Project. There are many ways to live a life, but one thing we know for sure though studying history, the arts, psychology, business, and nearly any field you wish is that there are certain characteristics to living a life of meaning and purpose. They also resonate with our country's founding ideals. I termed these self-evident truths the Civil Graces.

There are many graces to choose from, and incorporating even one or a few in your life is going to have an effect. The term *self-evident* means they are beyond needing proof. The goal is to live your life with intention and attention despite what is happening in the larger media context of the world. It is an invitation to get away from the noise and live the life you imagine and dream. This is a book about saving our world by first examining our own lives and putting these truths into practice.

This is not a new pursuit. Individuals who came before us have looked to find the meaning of life and to fulfill their purpose. Henry David Thoreau's writing in *Walden* always rang true for me: "If one advances confidently in the direction of his dreams, and endeavors to live the life which he has imagined, he will meet with a success unexpected in common hours." It is living with confidence—literally with "full trust"—that you can accomplish that vision of your life.

What will you discover on this path? That all you are searching for is within you, and this discovery can point to the keys for a more harmonious world. The real gift will be to yourself in that by embracing these graces, life will suddenly seem more gratifying, abundant, and your vision clearer.

Some people will dismiss what I offer—it is so much easier to point out there to what is causing the rifts in your life. The people in office, the economy, relationships, and what you had for dinner can all be reasons for anger and frustration. I assure you that we all try to pass the buck to avoid looking into the heart of the matter. Telling everyone about it on Facebook or Twitter doesn't help either. The reality is we can change the world simply by changing how we choose to see things.

When I was a kid, I had the sense to change things for the better—big and small things in my world were all an opportunity to make an impact. Having a curious mind about human potential, when I was ten years old, I read books like Dale Carnegie's *How to Win Friends and*

Influence People and John F. Kennedy's *Profiles in Courage,* and throughout my life, I looked to wise teachers exploring the meaning of life. In college, I graduated with degrees in political science, public policy, and women's studies because I felt the call to serve the greater good.

However, it was my work with the Fetzer Institute to discover what it means to have "freedom of spirit" that changed the trajectory of my life and the way I saw the world. As the president of the Institute at the time said, "Be the Thomas Jefferson of the spirit" and find out what is there. What an invitation! Over the years, those lessons have been swirling around in my mind, wondering in the context of all that I have learned: "What is my purpose?"

As a young woman, I lived my life, raised a family, and had a career. Through the triumphs, tragedies, and living the questions, I continually tried to stay open to what life was calling me to do. Finally, in 2017, I went after my dream: to serve the public and run for office. One could almost hear the herald angels sing! I was so excited that finally this was my time! All the signs were encouraging, and on April 19, 2017 (in honor of the first shots heard around the world of the American Revolution), I announced my candidacy for the U.S. Congress of the heavily gerrymandered Seventh District of Pennsylvania.

I could hardly believe how quickly the process dissolved before my eyes. The focus on everyone's mind was the money, and I wasn't raising it fast enough. My office was pressuring me due to politics there, and then friends and family turned their backs because they didn't like my ideas and where I stood on the issues. Everything that could go wrong did go wrong. I had to make a choice.

If it was meant to be, it was up to me, so I persevered. Connecting with the people was essential, so even with a tight budget, I found every way to reach as many voters as possible. The challenge with that was because of the distorted district, everywhere we went, people would say, "I love what you represent, but I am not sure if I am in your district."

People loved that I was authentically listening to them and hearing their concerns. They liked that I was not scripted and spoke from my heart. You *can* win without having all sorts of money—that is, if the powers that be will stay out of your way. Unfortunately, that is not what often happens. Despite the fact we were making great strides, there were too many trying to stop my race because I was an outlier who wanted to stand for the people.

Politics is not a sport for the fainthearted, but for more than a year, I gave my everything to this pursuit. My race ended after over a year of running when the State of Pennsylvania Supreme Court announced the unconstitutional gerrymandered districts would be redrawn. My district of five counties got reapportioned, which was good for the people, but like a game of musical chairs, my chair was gone, and my race was over.

Devastated doesn't describe how I felt. For months, I could hardly get myself to move forward each day. How could I recover from the loss a lifelong dream, not to mention all the sacrifices I made along the way? What was the purpose of my life if this wasn't it? I felt so incredibly vulnerable and lost. People kept telling me how much it meant to them that I ran and that by doing that much, I had made an impact, but I didn't believe that. I felt like a loser in life and a loser in my dreams. How could I have been so wrong?

Then I kept hearing that mantra: "If one advances confidently in the direction of his dreams, and endeavors to live the life which he has imagined, he will meet with a success unexpected in common hours." How could I find success, let alone get back on my feet? What was the meaning of all I had experienced, and how could I move on?

Bit by bit, the vision emerged. After seeing things evolve over time, I realized my work would come forth from that experience. The one thing that rang true to me again and again during my race was the power of the people and the strength that emerges from the connections we make with one another. None of us can make it alone, yet I saw firsthand how the influencers were trying to divide our country on almost any issue. We were losing the essence of what made us a great nation. Our diversity is our strength! I decided to explore that pursuit of finding the common ground.

In my search, I met with leaders in various fields, asking them about what they saw happening in the world. I was committed to finding out how still to have a role in making things better, but I knew it was not going to be in the position I had originally planned. One conversation in particular, with Dr. Martin Seligman, changed my thoughts. Learning of his groundbreaking work in positive psychology and resilience, I reached out to him. If anyone in the world could shed light on my situation, I hoped this expert would be the one. He wisely suggested that maybe there was another path for me. Perhaps the outcome of my race was not as bleak as I perceived it to be. In fact, he challenged me to take what I had learned and be "a trumpet of what is right in the world." How was I to do that?

I thought about the people I met along the campaign trail—people who were struggling in so many ways simply to exist. People who didn't feel heard or cherished, and people who felt alone. I met individuals of every walk of life who had such a desire to make things better and hoped for answers from their leaders.

In the debate and wrestle with the issues, I remembered one of the most poignant moments one evening after a long day. My husband, Vince, and I decided to stop at a local inn for a bite to eat and to take a break. There were very few people in the place at the time, so we ordered our food and hoped to have a quiet moment together. Suddenly I heard across the room, "So where do you stand on gun control?" One of the individuals across the way had seen my campaign badge and curiously wanted to know where I stood on one of the most controversial issues at the time. In the course of about an hour, I listened to his concerns and shared my thoughts. He served our country in the armed services; he wanted to know his family would be safe and that he could make sure that happened. I intuitively slid my chair from across the room in the course of this conversation until I was sitting across from this man. I saw the look in his eyes, and I understood. We both loved our country; we wanted our families to be safe. We simply disagreed about how that could be done. At the end of the discourse, he said, "Lady, I don't agree with all you have to say, but I would vote for you."

On one issue that easily could have divided us, each of us thinking we were right, we instead found common ground. I realized in hindsight that moment would reveal my work after the race ended. Sometimes when we lose in one area, we find there is another path that was meant for us.

My campaign was about being there for the people. In the end, supporters said, "There is always next time," but I didn't feel that. There was something early on that tipped me off, but I wasn't aware of it at the time. A pollster remarked after hearing why I was running said, "Go work with the UN and see if you can help change the world. You will be bored in Congress."

The thousands of dollars, steps in my shoes, miles on the car, handshakes, late nights, receptions, and debates were not lost because my vision of healing the nation and the world could still happen by helping people discover how everyone had the power to change the world even if it wasn't in an official capacity. I could take the moments like the one at the inn and bring them to light. There is more that unites us than divides us. I had to find a way to capture that so it could be applied to everyday life by everyday people, and with that, the Civil Graces Project was born.

We the people are the source of true power in this country. Want to start a march? Get the permits and organize. We have seen this happen again and again with growing momentum. I marched in so many rallies and was inspired by all the people I met along the way. Have a cause you believe in? Start a nonprofit, an organization, a small circle, or a business. Make T-shirts, sell stickers, write a blog, speak, and dream. In the words of the anthropologist Margaret Mead, "Never doubt that a small group of thoughtful, committed citizens can change the world; indeed, it's the only thing that ever has."

The Civil Graces Project is about focusing on uniting principles that uplift us and bring us together to pursue the common ground and make a more perfect union. It is about raising awareness of the civil graces that connect all people and celebrate the wonders of humanity. Those principles are exhibited in our work together and are found in our historical roots: hospitality, freedom, courage, generosity, and inspiration, among many more. At the end of this book, I left space so you can add your own. This is an ongoing project, and I hope you will join me.

Life is a celebration, and by bringing people together in our beautiful diversity with respect, we can transform the world one table conversation at a time. In the following chapters, we consider the etymology of the words when they were written or spoken centuries ago when our nation was coming to be. What was the inspiration that brought us together in the beginning? Maybe there are clues there on what we need today.

It is through the spirit of abundance, creativity, freedom, and joy that we can lift the barriers that try to divide human beings from one another and truly see one another as one in an indivisible wholeness. Together, we can address the global challenges we face and build a world with the opportunity for all to manifest a destiny of love, prosperity, and connection to the spirit of life.

In this day and age, when it feels that the global unconsciousness is leading the headlines, it is time for us to make a commitment to something better. We must raise our own energies and make the inner quest to do all we can to bring forth the civil graces and save the world from those who wish otherwise. It is up to us to change the way we think, what we choose to focus on, and to instead look to the questions of, "Who am I? What am I passionate about? How does this shape my relationships to whom and what I love? How then shall we live together knowing we all have a short time here? How may I live each day aware of these principles?"

What does it mean to show hospitality to one another? How do I display courage in my every day? How can coming from the heart of generosity bring more abundance than I ever knew? How can I live fearlessly and free in my life despite what reality displays? These are just some of the questions we will explore through our inner journey. We will reveal how focusing on what we believe can immediately create change and override the prevailing despair that seems to be shaping our current direction. The overwhelming feeling that "there is nothing one person can do" will be turned on its head as we perform small acts and embrace the power of our choice.

I welcome you to join me and explore the civil graces, looking to great minds who for all the ages have called to the human condition and seen a limitless universe that contains all we wish to be and who knew whatever we believed we could achieve was possible. The greatness in one of us exists in all of us, and together we can advance confidently in that direction to create the world that we only dreamed of in the past. Let us begin!

P.S., Regarding the meaning of the two thumbprints, we each have our unique identity, but if we are willing to come together with courage—literally with heart—we find common ground. It also is a tribute by its shape to the ancient symbol of the chalice explored by Riane Eisler in her ground-breaking work, *The Chalice and the Blade: Our History, Our Future.* If we are going to move forward, we need partnership and a return to equality and balance.

TRANSFORMING YOUR LIFE AND YOUR WORLD: AMAZING GRACE

> I do not understand the mystery of grace—only that it meets us where we are and does not leave us where it found us.
>
> —Anne Lamott

One of my favorite hymns growing up was “Amazing Grace.” I would listen to the tune and wait for the moment when amazing grace would teach my heart to believe.

> ’Twas grace that taught my heart to fear,
> And grace my fears relieved;
> How precious did that grace appear
> The hour I first believed!

I was always a sensitive kid and growing up defending myself with eight brothers and three older sisters often gave me a good reason to want to start a rebellion. Looking back, I never stopped feeling like it was my job to right the wrongs and save the world. I tried to make sure I made the road perfect, whether in my role as wife and mother, businesswoman and activist, or writer. It takes me days to work up the courage to write something. I work it over again and again in my mind before I can put words to print. Each time I do, grace appears.

The last several years have been transformative for me. I had to face that my first marriage was ending despite whatever we tried. The sadness at failing God, my family, and someone who used to be my partner was tremendous, but it was multiplied each time I looked into my children's eyes and tried to make things better despite all the statistics that said I would fail. My children are amazing. Statistics were wrong. Grace held us.

Then there was the time grace appeared to help me keep my home so that the kids didn't have to endure losing both their security and home at the same time. Grace appeared when I first believed via a promotion that gave me exactly (almost to the penny) what I needed to sustain the mortgage even though I had no idea how it would all work out. That house was our hideout from the world, a shelter in the storm that was raging in my heart.

Then I lost my father, who always felt like the one in my family who could truly see me. I know there was love, but to truly be seen was a gift. His absence from the world made me feel vulnerable beyond what I could remember. Going home the long road to Michigan the day after Christmas to say goodbye was complicated by a car that decided to act up. It was grace that allowed me to get through the icy roads to the safety of my childhood home, where I walked in line behind the legacy my father created.

Grace taught my heart to believe a few days later when a new friend asked me to a celebration at New Year's Eve. We had known of each other but had never spoken until he reached out to me on that lonely Christmas night after my dad had died to say I wasn't alone in my sadness; he had lost his dad at Easter. He knew what I was feeling on my first Christmas without Dad. Grace gave me the courage to believe in love again, and grace was right!

I had not ever lost my fighting spirit, and grace appeared to remind me about making a more just world. I answered what I felt was the call by running for the U.S. Congress. After all, there were no women from my state in Washington DC, and I knew what that meant: we would go hungry if we didn't get to the table and left it to the boys. After a year of running, changing my job, selling my beloved house, and almost losing my desire to live, grace once again met me with the words, "We aren't done with you yet." Though the last few years have been about finding a set of wings to fly because my feet were too tired to walk, grace has brought me safe thus far.

When my campaign experience was over, despite my grief and disbelief, it was looking to grace again that inspired me. The Civil Graces Project naturally emerged from the many instances during my race when I witnessed the human need to reconnect with one another in a world that seems to push us apart. We needed to re-member. Grace is the quiet presence of love and forgiveness, of not having the answer but waiting for the truth to emerge, and of having the courage to stay engaged with one another. Grace will transform our hearts, and I believe our nation and our world, if we remain open to that presence and one another.

THE CIVIL GRACES

HOSPITALITY

Etymology: From the Latin word *hospes* meaning "host, guest, or stranger." Also, *hospitalis*; Old French *hospitalite*; late Middle English *hospital*, *hospitality*; "a guest chamber."

> In the end, what's most meaningful is creating positive, uplifting outcomes for human experiences and human relationships. Business, like life, is all about how you make people feel. It's that simple, and it's that hard.
>
> —Danny Meyer

While growing up in a family with twelve children, I learned that anything significant happened at the table. We had a huge table that was originally my great-grandmother's. My parents had rescued several chairs from a nearby schoolhouse that had closed, so everyone (including visitors) had a place at the table. My mom would say, "We'll just add space for more." Everyone was welcomed—neighbor kids, relatives, and even kids from faraway lands I had never heard of but who had no place for the holidays in between college break would find room at our table. A few rules: Don't sit in your brother's spot lest you get a punch in the arm. Clean your plate because there are people in the world who are starving. And for goodness' sake, if you want something to eat, you'd better not be late!

The table was the center of our celebrations and life experiences. I will forever remember that spirit of sharing and welcome while growing up. We kids would hang on the words of any visitor because new ideas were as exciting to us as another serving of dessert! I knew from an early age that I wanted to be a mover and shaker, so mature people had me transfixed. What was out in the world, and how could I grow up quickly so I could be a part of it? Like Jimmy Stewart's character in *It's a Wonderful Life*, I wanted to see the world.

The gift of hospitality was more than offering a second helping; it was about the invitation to be with one another. As the traditional symbol of breaking bread, it was a time to put odds aside and share in an ancient ritual of feeding not only the body but also the larger purpose of connection. Hospitality became an art form. Opening my heart and home to make room for a friend or even a stranger is great fun and comes naturally for me. My husband and I enjoy hosting events throughout the year at our farm around a big table that I had built to resemble the one of my childhood. To us, there is always room at the table.

Consider the word *hospitality*. It shares the same roots as the word *hospital*, which is a place where we go to be healed. How often can our tables be a place of healing for the weary soul instead of an area of argument, upheaval, and judgment? The spirit of hospitality asks us to look again at the stories of old—where the one who welcomed and cared for the foreigner was revered and praised. Hospitality is an invitation to enter into this ancient art of healer and bring people together despite our differences so we can be nourished.

In my tradition, the idea of the loaves and fishes was as much a miracle of the teacher who shared it as it was of the people who opened their hearts to give what they had to the larger whole that all were fed. We are always blessed when we welcome the stranger (even if it means welcoming someone whose opinion we don't share) and make room at our table (even if that "table" is a park bench or the willingness to listen with an open heart of curiosity).

Hospitality is the first of the civil graces because I believe when we come together in a place to heal, we open ourselves to the abundant universe, which always gives despite our mishaps. I once heard motivational teacher, Wayne Dyer, speak, and he shared an ancient poem by Hafiz: "Even after all this time, the sun never says to the earth, 'You owe me.' Look what happens with a love like that. It lights the whole sky." We are invited to light up the world by this quiet grace of hospitality and make room in our hearts, our minds, and our spirits so we all have a place at the table, where we will find the beautiful gift each of us brings. These gifts become the balm to a world that needs each of our medicines.

One of the most amazing moments I had at a restaurant was at Gramercy Tavern in New York City. I deliberately wanted to see what was there because I had read Danny Meyer's book on hospitality and thought there was something magical about the way he saw his business. It was an extraordinary experience to behold. Everything was done in the art of caring for the patrons, right down to the fresh cloth towels in the bathroom. In the fashion of Disney's "Be Our Guest," every need was met with a smile. It left such an impression on me in a world where efficiency and cost-effectiveness almost always ruled the way business was done. On top of it all, one didn't have to pay extra for service—it was included.

We are in a world that is so quickly paced and driven that we miss out on the subtlety of the spectacular. Too many people rush in the door and race to the next event, all in the name of being well-rounded and fulfilled. Sometimes we forget to make time for hospitality.

It is a well-known fact that our oceans and environment are full of islands of plastic—signs of a "life of convenience." We often forget the elegance and grace of setting the table with the real dishes, the silverware, and the linens. There is something special about feeling like a guest at dinner and savoring an excellent meal. It is, as my husband, Vince, and I say, another way of making love. We give what we have and enjoy taking the time to really experience the moment. After having had loved ones pass all too quickly, we learned early on how life flies by. If you don't slow down to savor such moments, then what is life about?

Turn off the news, set aside the phone, get rid of all distractions, and treat yourself to real hospitality. If you live alone, it is okay. Lavish it upon yourself and dream of the life you imagine. When I was alone, I used to sit at the table and imagine what it would be like to share that experience with another, and when friends were available, I would often have a dinner party that went late into the night. The laughter and stories we shared trail back to my early childhood memories: the hours lingering luxuriously around a table and feeling the heartbeat of the rhythm of the hours.

As a mom, I subscribed to the idea that having dinner together would keep my kids from trouble, so dinnertime together was mandatory, much like it was for me growing up. There is a sense of connection with the day that cannot be captured any other time. I was a single working mom for many years while they were growing up, so life was less than what I would call perfect, but I still tried what I could to bring everyone together. Sometimes dinner was macaroni and cheese, and sometimes it was special if I had time and money, but dinner was always a sacred thing before the day came to a close. It was a ritual that let them know, "I see you, and I want to know what happened in your day." My favorite questions were to ask them what they saw that was beautiful. Usually they would say something to be funny, but it also let me know that we were doing okay.

The gift of hospitality is the genuine connection between human beings that keeps us going. The idea of someone waiting for you lets you know you always have a home. There is something so visceral about knowing you are needed that warms the heart and keeps you safe in the broader sense.

Imagine a world where we all met each other with such hospitality—where we found curiosity and excitement in meeting new people and hearing their views of the world without being offended. Imagine hurrying to not be late because we knew our presence was essential to the party of life, and knowing we were wanted and needed. This is possible when we embrace the civil grace of hospitality and see what happens when we make time and space for one more.

Reflection

Set your table. Use real dishes, silverware, glasses, and napkins if you have them. If not, improvise! What does it feel like to treat yourself and those you cherish a little extra special? Add an additional place setting to symbolize being open to having space at your table for the stranger or the one who needs healing. See what happens. Maybe someone will stop by and join you unexpectedly. Perhaps simply having that awareness will remind you to remain open to life and to anyone who comes to you. Life is all about savoring the moments, so no matter what you have, let it heal those places in your heart.

COURAGE

Etymology: Latin cor meaning "heart;" Old French *corage*; Middle English *courage*; "of the heart" or "seat of feelings"

> When the whole world is silent, even one voice becomes powerful.
>
> —Malala Yousafzai

Courage has often been understood as bravery and having the strength to do something extraordinary. We think of movie scenes when the hero or heroine is backed up against the wall but finds that last bit of gumption. *Cor-age* is Latin for "of the heart" or "coming forth with your whole heart." Ironically, the heart is sometimes negated as being weaker when compared to the mind. There is nothing braver or stronger than revealing your full heart, and the importance of carrying that message forth is why courage is one of the civil graces.

Who are you really? That is the most important question to answer in your life. In a world overwhelmed with mantras of success and social acceptance, showing up as you are is precisely what is needed. As children, we are often rewarded by our parents, churches, and educational institutions for being what was expected of us. Personally, there was always something nagging inside me that there was a different path. There came a time when holding on to that programmed version of myself was too painful. I had to rediscover my voice and remember my heart. Finding the courage to do that has not always been easy, but it has made my life more authentic.

Each of us emerges from the universe with unique gifts. Courage is the energy that moves it forth. To come from a place of the heart, a place of love and passion, is why we are here, and we must be persistent in bringing ourselves forward.

Courage invites us to show up each day. In a sense, it reminds me of our barn cat, PetE, who every morning peers in the window door looking to connect with us after a night of exploring. He doesn't necessarily want to come in but wants us to come out in his world. Again, and again, he invites us to experience what is real outdoors, and he won't be ignored.

There have been many times when I felt like I was hit with an emotional two-by-four, and it brought me to my knees. Divorce, loss of loved ones, sickness of children, losing dreams, and losing lifelong friendships have been some of the hardest times. Failure is such a tricky thing—we learn the most from when we try and fail, but often this is such a lonely road. Seldom does anyone want to be with the one who is down, and there is a time when positive thinking is not helpful. You cannot speed the process of grieving or healing, but when you have reached that point where you know you must go on, it has been courage that has helped me get back on my feet.

We are in a time where the sound bites and tweets are made to stoke the fires rather than to offer any solutions. I watch for leaders to emerge who will show genuine love for those they serve. It is rare to see them featured, but they are there. They may not have official titles, but there are individuals everywhere bringing all they are to tell their stories and bring meaning to life. Jane Goodall is someone I deeply admire—her courage to enter the jungle in Gombe and observe the lives of the chimpanzees who resided there is incredible. She speaks about the importance of our relationship to the world we live in with such grace and urgency. She went to understand how primates lived and came back with deep wisdom to share on how we are so interconnected with the natural world.

Jane's work inspired another more recent example in Greta Thunberg, who as a young woman stated her case with such profound courage to people of incredible power. Her heart was in every word, and it was such a sign for the world to do the same.

These women had a vision of speaking up for the Earth, and millions in the world were moved to stand out as well because they felt it in their own hearts. Malala Yousafzai stood up for education even though her very life was threatened. Her challenge to global leaders impacted girls around the world. That is the power of courage. We can ignite the world with passion toward a common goal. There is also a chance that you may never know who was inspired by your life, but you should follow your heart anyways!

We are heirs to the grace of courage. The original founders of this nation, leaders from every walk of life, had the vision that we could govern ourselves in a new way. It has taken centuries to reveal and reshape the ideal of self-government, but it has been through individuals calling out from their hearts to remind and remember something exists greater beyond the material world. The call is there for each of us. How do you show up in courage?

Reflection

Spend time contemplating the question, "Who am I?" What comes up for you? Write it down—even if it takes some time. What is inside of you that you may be afraid to bring forth? Is it a dream you have held, or a weight you want to release? Write it all down. Take a breath. Come back to what you wrote and explore where the civil grace of courage can be a tool to help bring your whole heart into your life.

CONFIDENCE

Etymology: Latin *confidentia,* from *confidere*; "to have full trust"

> Life is not easy for any of us. But what of that? We must have perseverance and above all confidence in ourselves. We must believe that we are gifted for something and that this thing must be attained.
>
> —Marie Curie

When you are born into a huge family, people often say strange things to you as a kid.

"God bless your mother! She must be a saint!"

"You must be Catholic!"

"Didn't your family have a television?"

"The winters must have been cold that year."

As I get older, these are somewhat humorous statements. Everyone was dancing around the issue of all those babies! I know my parents loved me, and all in all, I turned out okay. As a child, though, it sounded like a subtle way of saying, "You were a mistake, a burden, or something the Pope made happen." In short, "You weren't necessarily wanted."

Now, every kid has their issues. Only children and oldest children feel the weight of the world on their shoulders to perform, and they often feel the need to control. Middle children (of which I was one of the ten in my family!) feel like they are overlooked. And don't even get me started on the baby! As many things can, this perception took a toll on my self-esteem while growing up. I wisely learned to mask it as a desire to do great things simply to be noticed and deemed worthy. It was a gift in some ways. I was a reasonably good kid, straight As all the way, and an overachiever. My parents had it pretty easy because secretly, I was afraid that I might be a burden to them.

I have wrestled with the other side of this perception as well. It translated into something our society is also attached to: the art of perfection. If I am perfect, if I achieve great things, if I look the right way, then maybe I will earn my place. Perhaps then I will be worthy. So, you run after love in all the wrong places, take jobs you don't enjoy, shop trying to fill the swiss-cheese holes in yourself, or give away your time for free. We all have ways to numb those sore spots in our lives. Fortunately, I have often turned to meditation and creative pursuits like writing to do my soul work. I also have a thing with shoes—the higher, the better!

After much reflection, I suspect that the whole dream to run for office was also a manifestation of that energy. No one else but my dad got into politics, so it was one-on-one time and attention with him as well as the idea that I could save the world from its malaise. Whether it was war, poverty, injustice, or simply growing up through the seventies, I had lots of reasons to think that would be the ultimate calling. I could be a hero and transform the world! What I was looking for in all these efforts was to discover my confidence. I had to learn to have full trust in the purpose of my life beyond what I tried to do in the external world.

After my campaign experience was over, with all the time and money seemingly spent for nothing, I felt like I lost a lifelong friend. I mourned for many months afterward. Part of that sadness was the reality of what I experienced, and that is a whole other book how corrupt the process is. But in a real way, it was about saying goodbye to the idea that I would never be what I thought I needed to be worthy. I was sad that I felt I had to put myself through that in the first place, but on the flip side, I was the loser in the race. Having to wade through that dichotomy was not a swift process. In the end, the grace of confidence was there with a message: *You have been all you needed to be all along.* I simply needed to trust it.

When you experience major setbacks or life-changing situations, it can feel like you have to relearn who you are. Long ago, I had a friend survive cancer, and he said after all he'd lived through, he couldn't go back to life as he knew it. He was forever changed. When it is the death of a loved one or a dream, or tragedy of any kind, not knowing who you are can be so overwhelming on top of the grief you are trying to get over. *Confidere* ... to come with faith when you have no evidence that there is a resolution for the puzzle in your mind is one of the hardest things we have to work through. Even though it is cloudy, a rainbow will appear, and you will find your path.

I cried my way through the next election cycle. My heart was too tender even to see anything about who was running or winning. I'll never forget coming home from work that election day and looking up in the sky over my home. Across the sky was a majestic rainbow. All my angels were conspiring to let me know it would all work out; something else was waiting for me. Later that fall, I was walking next to the ocean, and I have a ringing ear that makes it hard to hear at times. In that ear, I clearly felt the words, "You will be compensated." I couldn't imagine what that meant, but for a kid who has been searching for meaning, how many more signs did I need to know I was enough? We all are enough.

The process of life and the humans we encounter can shape the lenses through which we see our world. The dynamic process of uncovering why you are here in the first place is sometimes elusive. Joseph Campbell, the great mythologist and writer, talked about the hero's journey that each of us is on—the call to adventure, refusing that call at first, initiation into it, meeting and defeating our demons, and returning to tell the story. We have to enter the places we most fear, because as Campbell stated, "The cave you fear to enter holds the treasure you seek." By entering into the cave, we discover that grace of confidence that pushes us further. We realize we have all we need inside us.

This is hard stuff to accept in a culture like ours, which seems so driven to get more and be more. It is challenging to emerge from experiences without victory. It was the loneliest time I can ever remember, but in one magic moment, I realized I had found a treasure. My son, Jack, openly said on the way to school one day, "Thanks, Mom, for teaching me how to go on after failure." While fighting back the emotions as he got out of the car, I felt that amazing presence—*confidere,* confidence—with full trust that we are always on a journey to self-revelation and to find those self-evident truths within ourselves that unite us with all of life. We are continually being compensated as long as we are willing to stay open long enough to let it shine through.

Reflection

Find a space where you can have some quiet and time to explore your heart. Close your eyes and envision that cave in your life you may be afraid to enter. Observe the feelings that arise within you. Ask yourself what might be the treasure waiting for you. Breathe deeply. See yourself taking that first step, knowing you can trust that you will find it. The journey will be worthwhile. You are worthwhile. Open your eyes and write down what you saw. Make ready for the journey ahead!

GENEROSITY

Etymology: late Middle English denoting nobility of birth; from Latin *generositas*, from *generosus* meaning "magnanimous" (from *magnus*, great and *animus*, soul)

> The meaning of life is to find your gift. The purpose of life is to give it away.
>
> —Pablo Picasso

From all that I have researched and observed, each one of us comes into life with a great soul or spirit. Even Epictetus, a Roman slave in the fourth century, admonished, "Why then are you ignorant of your noble birth?" Our presence in this world is more than simply acquiring lots of stuff and getting intoxicated with life's experiences. I believe a life worth living is to find the gifts we have within, or our purpose, and to spend our lives expressing that in whatever form inspires us. When we have a reason for being, or as the French beautifully say, *raison d'être*, the grace of generosity comes to life. French feminist philosopher Simone de Beauvoir once wrote, "That's what I consider true generosity: You give your all, and yet you always feel as if it costs you nothing."

Being generous comes from a space of abundance—not necessarily that you have enough, but that you trust there is always going to be enough, that you are enough. In a world where the idea of lack is so pervasive, this is a foreign concept to many. "If I give to you, then I will have less." For the essential things in life, this simply is not true. There is a statement that expresses this: "Equal rights for others does not mean less for you. It's not pie." Yet crafty politicians are able to use this fear of not enough to create division between people and misdirect funds toward war that could better be served by solving the issues of conflict like poverty, disease, and access to water.

The civil grace of generosity is more than giving and being kind. It is a way of life that involves trust in the goodwill of humanity. Despite what we are told and taught in school; the course of human history is dominated by good people simply trying to live a life of meaning. Most of us never could imagine harming another, yet those who do often get center stage in news accounts until we fear each other. Generosity reminds us to look to our noble nature and seek that in one another. We are called to rise to our best nature, and when we do, that is what will be mirrored back.

There are so many organizations around the world looking to bring people together and resolve the issues we face through the heart of generosity. Simply close your eyes and think of that. There are over seven billion people on the planet, and so many are going about their day to provide for their loved ones, make an impact, and find their purpose. The spiritual leader Ram Dass, whom I had the pleasure of meeting many years ago and who recently passed, had a saying: "We are all just walking each other home."

Imagine a world where we all remembered the spirit of generosity in each other. We would give from a deeper sense without looking to what is in it for us. We would not feel unworthy when another gives to us because we know that we may someday be able to return the favor. Perhaps this all sounds too altruistic, but consider the alternatives—keeping score, fearful living that results in human right abuses, war, and lack. I certainly don't wish for that world.

By the same token, you cannot pour from an empty cup. It is important that we replenish ourselves in order to be able to give. When we are depleted and stressed, it is nearly impossible to connect with the spirit of generosity. Ironically, it is through giving that we receive. This is not a quid pro quo arrangement; rather, when we give what we can, we often receive so much more back, even if it is a smile or a thank-you. We feel better about ourselves, and isn't that why we strive so much in life? We all want to feel happiness. Generosity, or remembering our noble purpose in the world, can quickly transform our lives and reconnect us to that feeling of true happiness and one another like nothing else.

In this country, we hold the ideal that all are created equal. We cannot hold this space of equality unless we are willing to be generous and realize that every person on this planet is worthy and beautiful and deserves to be treated well. America has long believed itself to be the best hope for humanity. It is time to remember how we can continue our work together and to live up to our words. Despite the diversity in how we each see that happening, there is room for it all when we remember our original nature.

Generosity makes space for the healing that needs to happen. It doesn't mean you have to change who you are to fit in, but by loving who you are despite what family or friends say, you recognize you are more than a human having a life experience. The civil grace of generosity invites us to truly see who we are, find kindred spirits, and connect with those throughout the world.

Reflection

Consider that you are of noble birth with a reason for being here. How does that make you feel? Is it a new concept for you, or is this something familiar? Carry that energy of being enough into your day, and at the end of the day, reflect how that has affected the way the day has unfolded. Remember your noble birth. Be aware of the company you keep. My dad would ask, "Why do you want to hang with the turkeys if you were meant to soar with the eagles?"

FREEDOM

Etymology: Old English *freodom,* "power of self-determination, state of free will, emancipation from slavery, deliverance"

> Between stimulus and response there is a space. In that space is our power to choose our response. In our response lies our growth and our freedom.
>
> —Viktor E. Frankl

Shortly after college, I had the incredible opportunity to work for a highly respected foundation, the Fetzer Institute in Kalamazoo, Michigan, which was on the leading edge to integrate the secular and the sacred to create a more loving world as well as promote healing in the world. My particular assignment was to explore what the founder, John Fetzer, meant by the term "freedom of spirit." Thomas Jefferson had expanded the meaning of political freedom, and I was to be the Thomas Jefferson of the soul.

Simply stated, I loved my work! I sat with spiritual leaders and elders from around the world, peppering them with questions, and they would often chuckle at my intense curiosity. I was still so young and eager. I soaked it all up like a sponge. How liberating it was to hear all these concepts and ways of living! It was another thing to be able to articulate it back to the larger circle of the organization, and it was even more challenging to explain to the outer world what I did for a living. I will never forget sitting at a dinner party and having someone ask, "So what exactly do you do?" Holistic living had not yet been revealed to the mainstream. People often chastised my work as merely crazy, a waste of time and of a degree.

I spent several years pouring through manuscripts and ancient texts, attending gatherings around the country (everything from sitting inside a kiva in the Earth, to native sweat lodges, meditation circles, yoga classes, and healing modalities of every variety), as well as sitting with accomplished authors and philosophers. It has taken most of my life to truly understand the spirit of freedom. Every day, something comes forth that reminds me of what I once heard or saw, and in a different context, the sense of freedom comes to life in a whole new way.

The quest to discover freedom's meaning is a journey we all are on, and although there are significant aha moments, there are also the struggles with freedom's opposites. As challenging as those times can be, they are our best teachers about deepening into the wholeness of all of life.

That is the mystery freedom reveals: as much as we believe we are separate, we are liberated when we realize we are all part of the universal breath that is in everything. What we do to another, we truly do to the collective self. Those who founded our nation understood those principles in the words they wrote: "All men are created equal." But we all know that even as those words were uttered, they were incomplete not only in missing the other half of the population, but also in their application because when they were written, humans were enslaved, and the rights of the indigenous people were ignored.

Our nation continues to wrestle with accepting the equality of all people. I believe we will be incomplete until we do. Seriously, what do we have to lose? Acknowledging the fullness of another doesn't take anything from your existence. Rather, it aligns you with the fullness of who you are.

One of the most profound teachers on freedom was Viktor Frankl. Though I never met him, I read his books in tears and quiet awe for how a human being could withstand so much torture, sadness, and destruction as he did in the Holocaust yet still come forth without bitterness. He took what he witnessed in all its horror and showed us a pathway to true freedom.

Life holds deeper meanings, even when we are going through the most horrible circumstances. Regardless of what we are enduring, life is calling us to where freedom is always available—through our thoughts and the choices we make. Our ultimate freedom is deciding how we shall see the world—as Frankl stated, "to choose one's attitude in any given set of circumstances, to choose one's own way."

His words have a profound meaning for us, especially today as we wrestle with the current political and social climate in our world.

> It did not really matter what we expected from life, but rather what life expected from us. We needed to stop asking about the meaning of life, and instead to think of ourselves as those

> who were being questioned by life—daily and hourly. Our answer must consist, not in talk and meditation, but in right action and in right conduct. Life ultimately means taking the responsibility to find the right answer to its problems and to fulfill the tasks which it constantly sets for each individual.
>
> —Viktor E. Frankl, *Man's Search for Meaning*

If anyone could endure the suffering that Frankl and so many did in the Holocaust and come back with such vision, then what is freedom calling forth in each of us now? How can we ignore those lessons? It is time to remove the scales from our hearts and feel the connection we have with each other.

We all are on a continuous journey to the civil grace of freedom. The challenge is that freedom in our culture has been mostly focused on doing rather than being. It has been interpreted as to do whatever one wants, financial freedom, social freedom, religious freedom … all of which can be taken away in a moment. When I speak of freedom as a civil grace, I am inviting you to consider the freedom that no one can touch, yet it will transform your life in a way that the others cannot. When the spirit of freedom enters in this way, we find we become more open and accepting and less threatened by external realities. Then when we have alignment within, we have the strength to stand up and work to bring that to other aspects of life. We live in the present moment without holding onto the past or fear of the future.

As a mom with growing young adults, the issues of freedom and independence is present every day. My children were babies just moments ago, and now they are finding their wings and their voices. Holding space for the spirit of freedom as it lifts off is the ultimate act of love. "I hope you have all the tools you need to find your path and stay on your course." We cannot navigate our children's hero's journeys for them.

A word that we use synonymously with freedom in our culture is liberty. We say we believe in "liberty and justice for all," and if this is our true ethos, then we have to expand the field of what is acceptable in our world. There are more answers than just one. There are many ways to live life and express love. Our desire to have our freedom must coexist with one whose expression may not be our own. When we rise above the *doing* aspect of freedom and open our hearts and minds to *being* free, there is space for it all. We continue to expand ever upward, and when we can truly embrace this understanding, we find healing and meaning in everything we encounter.

We begin to see the light in each other, and with this understanding, we find all the other graces that lead us to a more loving and peaceful existence with all of life, including our planet. When we stop the war within ourselves, the ones outside of us also dissipate. When we experience the freedom within, we are enough, and because we aren't hoarding out of lack, there is enough for everyone.

We all have lived through disappointments and despair in various degrees. No matter how we run from it, that is the essence of life—the joy and sorrow sit side by side, the light and dark follow one another, and just as the waves come in, they depart back into the ocean. If we are fixated on controlling life, we can get battered and bruised. However, if we go to where our center is and decide no matter what situation comes before us, we will be free, there are no bars that can hold us back.

Meditation, yoga, walking in nature, music, writing, creating—all these are vehicles to help us get close to that essence of Freedom within us. It has been in exploring my own stillness that I have found my voice again so I may write my story, and each time, freedom brings a gift of understanding to a new part of myself that I hadn't seen. When I am in a calm state of mind, I have created space to have time to consider how I will respond. When I choose stress, it is easier for me to come from hasty words and decisions. You don't need elaborate exercises or subscriptions to anything in order to meet the freedom within. You have all you need right here and now.

Relationships to those who are closest to us have been strained in our current debate. We see ourselves split over disagreements on what "we the people" should be doing, whom we vote for, and who is right and who is not. Heated words spoken online that we would never say face-to-face weigh heavy the minute they are expressed, and at times I have reflected on what I had written and found myself hitting delete. That is not who I want to be.

Freedom invites us to step back from the immediacy of the moment, take a breath, and realize we cannot control another—nor do we need to. There is space for it all, and the debate can be grist for the mill to lead us to a better place—that is, if we are willing to do the inner work on ourselves first.

If we step back and stay open to what each moment is teaching us regardless of what it is, we have a better chance at expressing our freedom to choose our response. Do we come with fear or love? This single act of choosing is our greatest power.

Every day, embrace being a student to life—what some traditions call the beginner's mind. Create a space to invite the civil grace of freedom into your being ... then get ready to expand and be transformed!

Reflection

Take a walk outside in nature if you are able; if you are not able, close your eyes and envision being in nature. Explore all the different textures, colors, and expressions in the flowers, trees, and scenery around you. Notice how each coexists and the freedom of it all. Know that this is your essence too. Write down what that feels like in a journal and ponder how to bring that spirit into your day.

HUMILITY

Etymology: Latin noun *humilitas* or adjective *humilis*; "humble, grounded;" from the root word *humus*; "earth"

> There is nothing noble in being superior to your fellow man; true nobility is being superior to your former self.
>
> —W. L. Sheldon

Did you ever do something as a child and get grounded? If you are like most pioneers who stepped outside the box, I am sure you did! It always was a funny phrase for punishment: "You are grounded." As an adult, I am continually striving to be in the mindset of grounded-ness through meditation and reflection. The gift of grounding ourselves allows expansion of our awareness and reveals the profound truth that we are all playing our part in the *uni-verse*, or one song.

In my tradition, we learned as children we are of the earth to return to the earth—*humus,* which is the soil formed by all that has broken down and rotted to create the place where new things grow. A word that springs from the word *humus* is *humility.* Things grow, including life-nourishing gifts from the humus of our lives.

Humility is a civil grace not because we are called to be lower than the dirt but because we are called to embrace life with wonder and be grounded in the knowledge that we belong here. There is something essential about our very nature that we came into being in this time and space.

Humility allows us to realize that maybe we don't have all the answers. Life is about living in the mystery of the questions, and the most important questions we can answer are, "Who am I? What ignites my passions? What does this mean to all my relations to the people in my life, to my work, and to my world?" Can you imagine a world where we all lived from our true essence, from a space of humility and wonder?

I can imagine that we would try less to impress and possess. We would be open to solutions and would be able to recognize them when they presented themselves. We live on a planet that scientists believe to be over 4.5 billion years old and in a universe that exceeds our ability to comprehend time and space. Physicists believe we came from elements of stardust connected to all of the atoms of our galaxy, and there is a more profound connection we all share, including to our natural world.

We are experiencing times of significant change when the old systems of a controlling culture—our institutions and ideologies—no longer seem to be working. Something new is emerging, and people around the globe are asking, "Is there a better way?"

When looking at the surface, it can be overwhelming. Yet according to the mathematical ratio, the golden proportion, although things may seem in chaos, the solution is there. Everything expands upward and eventually reaches harmony, including us. A common example of the golden proportion is the cross-section of a nautilus shell. Each section curves into a larger sized section of the same design, and this pattern creates an ever-increasing space. Sunflowers have this same pattern in their centers. It is everywhere once you start to look for it, including in all of us. Our very nature is expansion. Like most of life, we live in the dichotomy of things—simplicity and complexity. In it all, we are evolving to an ever-increasing awareness that we can trust. The pain comes when we resist growth.

Humility invites us to go deep within, get grounded in our core. It invites us to not be swayed by the winds that swirl around but to explore our inner spirit. “What is this all about, and how can I help?” It is the call to see another dichotomy that we live in the world but are not of it. We share our very nature with all of life on the planet and therefore have a responsibility to take care of it. In the end, we are soil and stardust. We are both common as mud and as grandiose as the universe.

Reflection

We are all soil and stardust. Take time to consider the grace that humility brings and our connections with all living beings. Consider your life and how your actions and habits affect the planet. With mindfulness and in consideration of this relationship, commit to making at least one change in how you live your life to improve the environment.

EQUALITY

Etymology: Latin *equ* meaning "equal;" *aequalitatem* "equality, similarity;" from *aequalis*, "uniform, identical in size, equal likeness;" Old French *equalité*, "equality, parity;" Originally was a term used in trade to mean things were of uniform size or same amount to insure fairness.

> No matter what message you are about to deliver somewhere, whether it is holding out a hand of friendship, or making clear that you disapprove of something, is the fact that the person sitting across the table is a human being, so the goal is to always establish common ground.
>
> —Madeleine Albright

After the election in 2016, our country was up in arms over the outcome. There were all sorts of comments about the other side, about people who were different, and about the great divide we were entering. Regardless of whom you voted for, I think you can agree we have grown a bit more contentious as a nation over the last few years.

Despite how it may show up, however, I believe we all love our country. Because of our immense experiences, we see things differently. It is this variety of ideas and opinions which has always led us to new solutions and advancements. When I bring my authentic self to connect to your full being, we create something new in between us. It becomes not “me-or-you” but a third option--us. In this connection with one another, we are transformed. If we are willing to see it, this is where we can align because we are more alike than we are different. As human beings, we share so much in common. Alfred Lord Tennyson reflected, “I am a part of all that I have met,” and when we see this common thread that joins all of us, we discover space for the civil grace of equality.

Too often we are labeled by who we are, what we do, the money we make, or our views on any issue. We are continually defining and being defined. Some of this stems from our need to set boundaries in our minds. We know who we are when we see what we are not. Unfortunately, labeling also stems from fear of “the other.” If I don’t agree with you, and I label you as different from me or not right, then I can justify the way I feel and the things I think about you. Perhaps it doesn’t bother as much then when you are hurt or oppressed. That is the danger in the concept of the other.

As author of the novel *Beloved*, Toni Morrison wrote, “Definitions belong to the definers, not the defined.” We are not in control of the labels placed on us, and they tell less about us than the one who uses them. Nonetheless, when used to discredit or demean, labels inhibit our ability to see each other. When we group people under a label, it is easier to disregard them, and we lose connection.

Wayne Dyer often stated, "When you change the way you look at things, the things you look at change." This works as well for looking at people positively as it does when we are critical of them. The danger of labeling is that it is all about prejudice—literally meaning we prejudge someone before receiving them and close off the possibility for honest connection.

When I was running for office, I had specific labels attached to me because of my political stances, and individuals would decide whether I was a good or bad person on that alone. Even if they formerly liked me, I suddenly became a bad person with the wrong label. They never attempted to have a more in-depth conversation; they simply wrote me off. As a candidate, I found the most powerful thing I could do was listen and give people space to tell their stories. I leveled the field by opening my mind to the possibility that there might be something I could learn. When we made space and time, we could often find common ground.

We miss so many opportunities to connect when we prejudge. This happens again and again, especially when you are in the public arena, and people rely on what they get secondhand. It is like Hans Rosling stated: "Forming your worldview by relying on the media would be like forming your view about me by looking only at a picture of my foot." Although one expects it when running for office, is this what we want for our world in everyday life? Cutting ourselves off from each other because of prejudged labels? This limits the possibilities for our planet and resolution to our most pressing issues, including treating each other with equality.

One thing is for sure: we are all uniquely created. Right down to our fingerprints, we are stamped with our own identity. Every single one of us is influenced by nature and nurture, our physical and mental makeup as well as our spiritual and social environment. When you think of all the variables that go into a life, it is no wonder that we are so different and have so many viewpoints!

From one vantage point, this is incredibly profound. Think of the options and the diversity! But from a place of fear, differences sometimes hold us apart from one another, and often to feel safe, we use labels to define this and that, what we like and what we don't, what is right and what is wrong. Boundaries are a healthy way of knowing who and what you are—until the mind and heart are closed.

Part of the challenges today seems to stem from the fact that things are moving so quickly—time, information, and change. What we used to know as reliable and secure no longer feels that way, and understandably, we start to reinforce those boundaries when things don't feel right.

Yet nature teaches us another way: the way of expansion. If I am willing to grow in my understanding and ability to see alternatives, then what works for you and what you believe doesn't threaten me simply because we don't agree. There is space for both of us. That is the key. When we want so badly to hold onto our way and close out any challenge that may be perceived, we stop growing. We are here to expand and to continue to grow in all forms. That's why it feels so bad when we close down: it isn't our nature to do so.

When I was campaigning, I had a family member state they didn't like my issue platforms and that I most assuredly would pay the price for having those positions. It first offended me, but then I realized that I hit a cord with this person. It didn't mean I was wrong. It didn't mean the person was wrong in their mind. We simply didn't agree. Could I still love the person even though we were worlds apart on issues? The answer is of course I could. I couldn't change their view, and they couldn't change mine. However, we could respect each other as equals to know we are entitled to our own beliefs. It was great practice because I encountered this so often when being challenged on the issues. After a while, it didn't bother me so much. It made me a better leader to learn to hold that space for each of us to have a voice and ideas of our own.

When you feel insulted or offended by the things people say, the way they dress, or the ideas they have, ask yourself whether you can make space for both of you with the civil grace of equality. It frees you at the same time and makes room for options. We are never justified to be cruel to another, and most of us would never consider hurting someone else. But from time to time, we have to reflect on whether our ideas and boundaries are worth clinging to when we use them to separate, discriminate, and judge each other.

Leaders don't have to be elected officials. Everyday people like you and me can help reshape the dialogues in our communities. To make this happen, we are going to have to take some risks. What would it be like when we let go of labels and prejudging? Does it make us more vulnerable and possibly lead to confrontation? Maybe. But if we are willing to see each other equally as human beings, perhaps there will be an opportunity to experience something more profound. By reconnecting with each other on common ground, we can stop defining ourselves and others and find true freedom and equality at last!

Reflection

Pay attention to the way you speak and write about people and their ideas. Are you comfortable when someone doesn't share your thoughts? Do you take the opportunity to have others tell you more, or would you rather shut them down? Equality begins in our minds when we search for the common ground we share with all human beings. Invite yourself to the table. Recognize your place. Set the table wide and far. Welcome everyone you meet. Recognize each person's place alongside yours.

ATTITUDE

Etymology: The French word *attitude* originally was a seventeenth-century term in art to describe posture or placement of a figure; from Italian *attitudine*, *aptitudo*, "disposition, posture, fitness;" *aptitudinem*, "a posture of the body supposed to imply some mental state." Also used as a term to describe orientation in travel.

> It's not what happens to you, but how you react to it that matters.
>
> —Epictetus

My husband, Vince, flies airplanes for a hobby, and he often uses aeronautical terms to make a point. His favorite one is that if you have bad attitude, you are definitely headed for danger. It is the relation of the aircraft to the horizon of the Earth that determines attitude. When you are tilted downward or too high up, you are not in a good position to stay in flight. Literally, a bad attitude can cause one to crash and burn.

This analogy astutely points out the fact that our attitude greatly affects the outcomes of our lives. We need to remember no matter what is going on in the world, we are powerful beings who are able to overcome and find solutions to things that seem so challenging. The first step is to own the power of our thoughts and our choices. We need to carefully choose our attitude.

Attitude as a civil grace invites us to be aware of the state of our mind. Have you ever experienced when you are thinking about a thing, it seems to appear right before your very eyes? Attitude works with attraction in that what we place our minds, that is what we see. Your life is all about your attitude.

When I was a kid, my mom used to get tape recordings from the library of motivational speakers for background while she worked. The stories shared on these lectures were often entertaining, and I would curiously sit and listen while taking notes on the key points. Okay, so I was a strange kid, but human potential has always intrigued me. Even today, if you look at the books on my nightstand, they are mostly self-improvement, the power of the mind, and how to develop healthy mindsets. TED Talks, podcasts, and MasterClasses are something I still enjoy because this example was set early in my life—the idea that despite what we see as reality, there is always a way to change the world by changing the way we perceive it.

So many times I have been confronted, “Yes, but what about the situation of my life? I didn’t ask for this!” No one asks for challenging situations in our lives, yet every one of us will meet them. Where we are born and the physical, mental, social, and financial conditions of our lives are not always what we would choose. That is a common thread that unites us. The irony is that happiness and a truly successful life have little to do with external circumstances. I have met financially well-off individuals whose problems where unbelievable; likewise, I have met people who had very little but were living bliss. Get out there and find out for yourself if you don't believe me!

I will repeat this again with emphasis: The situation of your life has very little to do with external circumstances and everything to do with the state of your mind. The single most important determiner in your life is choosing your attitude, or as Ed Foreman, a popular motivation speaker, would say, "What side of the menu are you ordering from today?"

We have many examples throughout our nation's history of individuals who defied the odds and were able to make incredible contributions. These leaps would have been impossible if we weren't dreamers and believers. At our very core, we are inventors and explorers for deeper truths and opportunities. President John F. Kennedy wisely shared, "We have the power to make this the best generation of mankind in the history of the world or make it the last." It was his belief in what was possible that created the space for us to go to the moon. Now hold that spirit of imagination and know it will help launch your dreams as well.

We have a saying in our home: "What you think about, you bring about." Though there are times when I really don't want to hear this, I know in my heart it is true. I will see through the lens I choose, and life will follow my orders. There are many scientists studying this today through quantum physics and the power of the placebo effect. They will concur that everything great that ever happened started as an idea in someone's mind, and by staying in the field of possibilities, they are able to manifest their dreams and heal themselves in ways that blow the mind. This is the next frontier, and when I read about the possibilities, there really isn't anything to hold us back.

If your life or situation is not exactly what you love, ask yourself how you are in your position with your world. No one is going to do your work. Stop waiting for the one person to come along who is going to solve all your challenges. This is your journey. Those challenges in your life are invitations to discover who you really are. They are your teachers. The word *crisis* in the Chinese symbol is two words: danger and opportunity. Seize the day!

Reflection

We become what we think about all day long. For one week, track your thoughts in relation to your situation and how you feel. When you feel your nose dragging, try to find a reason to look up. Remind yourself that in every crisis, there is a choice—danger or opportunity. What do you choose?

AWARENESS

Etymology: Old English *wær* "wary, cautious, having knowledge or consciousness of something, state of being;" earlier word used *awaredom*

> A butterfly could flap its wings and set molecules of air in motion, which would move other molecules of air, in turn moving more molecules of air—eventually capable of starting a hurricane on the other side of the planet.
>
> —Andy Andrews

One morning as I was driving my son to school, I suggested he put down his device and look out the window at the full moon still resting in the early sky while the rosy haze in the east began to herald the sun. As if on cue, a herd of deer raced across the misty field, and a large crow made its perch in a tree along the road. Mother Nature was definitely in show-off mode with this young observer, and we quietly took in the moment.

Are we aware of the grace that surrounds us every day? Do we see the beauty despite the rush we are in to make our way to the next leg of our journey? Native cultures looked to our environment for direction and with anticipation for what came next. The cycle of the seasons, outer space in its orbit, and the weather have been linked to our own circadian rhythms, yet the modern world seldom slows down to reconnect and breathe these beats. Maybe this is why our environment is so easily disregarded by some: we have forgotten our interconnection and relationship to it. If you are feeling overwhelmed or simply need a break, take time to look at what surrounds you. Give gratitude for the beauty no matter how small, and if you haven't yet found anything to cherish, keep looking.

It can be hard to consider beauty when so many feel forgotten. The suffering around us doesn't make sense at first sight, and it is hard to see heaven in certain situations. Could it be that awesome forces are revealing something for all of us to see? At first glance, we may see pain and suffering. At second glance, we see that we are being summoned to reach beyond borders and beyond our own limitations to help our fellow neighbors, and to realize that we can create heaven here by the love that we share.

One exercise that was helpful in keeping centered in my life was to choose four words that were significant for me. My mentor, Caroline, knew I was going through an especially difficult time and said that by finding these core values, I could regain my balance. My words are abundance, creativity, freedom, and joy. I love abundance because then everyone has enough, and creativity because it is my soul's essence. I love freedom and hope everyone has access to it. Most of all, I love joy. Joy gives life meaning and helps us when its counterpart shows up. These words can change over time, but what I discovered is like the cardinal directions north, south, east, and west, my four words are like my inner compass. When I feel out of balance or loss, I can use creative expression to bring me back. My belief in abundance often leads me on scavenger hunts to find it is absolutely true. When I feel free, I feel joy. I can always find my true north by being aware of my core. It is like having four legs on a table: there is balance and a place to create.

Another form of awareness is *situational* awareness. Being cognizant of what is going on around us helps us identify opportunities, potential threats, or dangerous situations. In our modern world, this includes being discerning about information, how our data is collected, and sometimes used to manipulate public opinion. Situational awareness also helps us know when we, as a society, are ready to make a change. From time to time, we have let this awareness slip, and the result was pain and loss even though indicators were signaling that we needed to make adjustments, speak out, or take action. There are times when we forget what is essential. We don't want to rock the boat or slow the economy. We can get too far ahead of ourselves that we fail to perceive what is happening now, and the costs are often catastrophic. In the now is where our real power resides. We have to be willing to have full awareness in the present moment and then take inspired action to do what we can.

Awareness calls us back to our center. It asks us to show up fully in our being. What do you love? What makes your spirit soar? Write it down. Like Natalie Goldberg said, "write down the bones" so your dreams may have structure! Write your four words! Imagine if we each unplugged and did what we could. The invitation is there for each of us to reengage with our natural world and one another. One single drop in a pond creates ripples that reach the far-off shore as a wave. A flap of a butterfly wing contributes to the hurricane. What are you waiting for? Every conscious act you take can change the world for the better.

Reflection

As you move about your day, however you transport to your tasks at hand, take a moment to call yourself to awareness of what is around you. See how often you lose your train of awareness through the day, and gently call yourself back. What do you notice? Write your four core words that are directions that can lead you back to your center.

RESPECT

Etymology: Latin *respectus*, from the verb *respicere*, "to look back at, to regard"

> No tree has branches so foolish as to fight amongst themselves.
>
> —Native American proverb

Have you observed the headlines or the reposts on social media much? In an effort to stay "informed," I do check in each day. It was especially important when I was running for office to keep my finger on the pulse. So much of what we hear is we are a nation divided. We are reminded that we are in opposition and in competition with one another. Whenever I meet with people face-to-face or in small groups, this is not necessarily a reality. Are we really divided as much as all the hype says?

I am going to be bold and say no, we are not divided. We are diverse. Given our history, we have seldom agreed on how things should be done save for a few moments when we were collectively attacked. We have had heated debate and discourse from the very beginning. The current challenge is the breakdown in that discourse. Some leaders would very much like to see this alleged divide get deeper. When people are looking for a better way, those who would like to control use fear to paralyze and create animosity. It sells elections, the media, and gets us anxious.

When a nation is divided, it is much easier to overcome, but a united people are much harder to break, even if their ideas are diverse. If we are constantly told we are at odds, we begin to lose hope in one another. That is the real tragedy.

Abraham Lincoln wisely stated in his Inaugural Address, “A house divided against itself cannot stand.” It was Lincoln’s patience and wisdom that held our country together during one of our most challenging times, when the nation was divided between North and South over the rights of freedom for all people and the battle over states’ rights. Harriet Tubman was a guiding force during those times. She led people to freedom from bondage, and her words ring true today as they did when she crossed over into freedom from slavery: “When I found I had crossed that line, I looked at my hands to see if I was the same person. There was such a glory over everything; the sun came like gold through trees, and over the fields, and I felt like I was in Heaven.”

We have the invitation to cross over the line, listen to the many voices, and be willing to work to create a better world together. That was the dream of America: from many countries would come one stronger nation of self-governance. The people of this nation committed to ending the centralized control of one person (the king), and they endorsed the idea we could do this together. Our history is checkered with times when we have been heroic and at times cruel. The challenge is to find ways to grow beyond that, and the civil grace that will lead us there is respect.

The word *respect* is from Latin *respectus*, from the verb *respicere,* "to look back at, to regard." When we can look back and see the eyes of another and not see them as other but rather brother or sister, we realize that we need their ideas *and* our own. We cannot accomplish self-governing with one side any more than we can row a boat with one oar in the water; we will keep going around in circles.

I have a good friend who helps organize communities when disasters strike. She says it is amazing to see that when people are dealing with a crisis, we forget who is on what side of the aisle and who voted for whichever candidate. We come together as neighbors and work together to resolve the issues and rebuild the community. This happens every single day in a thousand communities across our country. When we remember our common humanity, we let go of the labels and help each other get back up when we are down.

Respect reminds us that there is more to life than amassing wealth and titles. It is about living a life that we can regard and the legacy we will leave behind for those who follow our footsteps. It is not about stoking the fires of political, religious, or cultural division to prove right is might, but rather seeking the call to find the common ground where we can begin anew each day with space for everyone at the table.

The headlines beat our minds, telling us that hate crimes and division are surrounding us and making us too afraid to speak out or to reach out to our neighbor.

Social media allows us to repost the outrageous instead of actually sitting face-to-face to dialogue with one another. Our leaders point the finger at the injustice of one side while three more fingers are pointing back at them.

Respect invites us to heal our own woundedness and see that our role is to be the voice of liberty for each other. There are many ways to be in the world, and there is proof of this all around us. When my kids were younger, I would point out the diversity in nature and remind them that there is not one tree or flower that is exactly alike. Each one is unique, beautiful, and diverse. That is what makes our world wonder-filled, and it is the same with people.

Some scholars believe we are living through a period of reckoning and reawakening—having to face ancient hatreds and sins of our past. The collective is being mirrored in the leaders in front of us. Do we like what we see? There are steps we can take to make things better, but the most important space to examine is our own hearts and minds.

Just as we may hold our truths to be self-evident, we must respect that others may hold other beliefs that are just as real to them. To demand that they conform to our answer is to make our world more violent and unjust. Again, I will say we are not divided. We are diverse. Having respect to make sure all are at the table and that each voice is heard is a way to find the common ground that still is there for all of us.

Reflection

Look into the mirror. Who do you see? What resemblances do you see? Consider all that happens in your life is a reflection of what you carry within you. We are all mirrors to one another. Practice bringing respect to all those you meet along the way.

GRATITUDE

Etymology: Late Middle English or Old French *gratitude*; or from Medieval Latin *gratitude*, "thankfulness, good will;" from Latin *gratus*, "pleasing, thankful;" *gratia*, "grace"

> Gratitude unlocks the fullness of life. It turns what we have into enough, and more. It turns denial into acceptance, chaos into order, confusion into clarity.... It turns problems into gifts, failures into success, the unexpected into perfect timing, and mistakes into important events. Gratitude makes sense of our past, brings peace for today, and creates a vision for tomorrow.
>
> —Melody Beattie

One powerful thing that has transformed my life faster than anything is the practice of being grateful. Every morning, I try to remember to say, "Thank you, thank you, thank you. I have another day." This simple prayer starts my day in the direction of service, and I believe my role is to give all I have in this life. This life is a gift, and at the end of my life, I want to have used up everything I have in myself. As the years pass and I look back at the things I overcame, the times I thought I would just die and didn't, I have two words: thank you.

Gratitude has been a cornerstone of my parenting and in my marriage. Starting from when they were small, I had my kids say one thing they were grateful for at dinner time each night. It isn't always so inspiring when you have teenagers who give you a glare and don't want to say anything, but it is a ritual we continue even to this day. Before we begin the day, my husband and I, despite whatever is before us, look at each other with the praise, "I am grateful for you." When we can find something for which to be grateful in our world and in each other, we show we have trust that all is well or at least is on its way. It goes beyond just appreciation; it is that sense of belongingness and sustaining our relationships with each other.

Benedictine monk David Steindl-Rast says, "Gratefulness is the key to a happy life that we hold in our hands, because if we are not grateful, then no matter how much we have we will not be happy—because we will always want to have something else or something more." This wanting something more is a phenomenon described in the Buddhist tradition as "the hungry ghost," the consciousness that is always roaming the world seeking for more and is never filled. This feeling of "never enough" is familiar in our Western society. We are bombarded by images of what we should look like, what we should have, how we need to behave … the list is endless. It tricks us into believing we are what we have and what we do. Then if we lose it all, we feel we are nothing. The civil grace of gratitude calls you back from the brink to remind you that you hold the key to happiness already. You have everything you need.

One thing that I heard a lot about when I spent time listening to people during my political campaign was their concerns over addiction and suicide, which continues to rise every year. Not a day would pass that I didn't meet someone who knew someone who had died from either suicide or addiction. It transcended any age or demographic, and their lives were deeply missed. We lost a nephew to suicide, something that carved a hole forever in my family's life. There isn't any way around the suffering except to try to listen to the lessons their struggle taught. I always wonder, Did he know how much he was loved? Did we let him know we were grateful for his presence?

I don't know how we solve that growing issue in our country, but I think about it all the time. How can we help transform the meaning in life so that it is more profound than just the material realm? How do we help our young people, our wounded people, those who struggle with mental health, and those who feel left behind? How do we make a culture where we are enough, and we are worth it? When you have loved ones who struggle with mental health or addiction, there are no simple answers, but one thing suggested through many resources is that the simple act of gratitude can be a step in the right direction.

Gratitude breaks down the walls of isolation, and it helps alleviate the notion that you are alone or different, which is what often leads to depression and addiction. With gratitude, you see that others are trying to help you, and that means you are loved. You don't have to go it alone. Gratitude can help you feel better physically and mentally, and it boosts your self-esteem as well as enables you to sleep better. The list of health benefits often makes me wonder why we don't do more to promote building gratitude in our society beyond one day in November.

Gratitude comes from the word *gratia*, which means grace. Pioneer French educator of the deaf Jean-Baptiste Massieu said, "Gratitude is the memory of the heart." It is a part of our core essence, which is why it feels so good to bring it forth! Grateful people are more in touch with their environment and the relations around them. It is a civil grace because, in the pure, free act of gratitude, we create a foundational safety net for all of us to live. When we are grateful, we feel our lives have meaning, and this leads to significant personal growth. It builds social bonds and trust in our communities. Gratitude invites us, in the words of Thich Nhat Hanh, to "Walk as if you are kissing the Earth with your feet." Every step is a blessing.

Reflection

Do you keep a gratitude journal? If not, start one. You can do it in the morning when you first arise, or at night before you go to sleep. Take time to reflect on five things for which you are grateful. Write them down. Feel free to write a note to those who make your world a better place; let them know you are thankful for them.

RESPONSIBILITY

Etymology: From the Latin verb *respondere*, "answered, offered in return;" French *responsible*, "answerable, accountable for actions, trustworthy, reliable"

> In the long run, we shape our lives, and we shape ourselves. The process never ends until we die. And the choices we make are ultimately our own Responsibility.
>
> —Eleanor Roosevelt

I like to play with the meaning of words, and you might have noticed that on each of the civil graces, I include a brief etymology of the word. It fascinates me how words evolve, and there are often deeper meanings to the ones we use. We usually don't consider what they meant back in the eighteenth century when the foundations of our democracy were being set forth. By looking at them more closely, we can find a new way to understand what they were trying to convey by the self-evident truths and how it could relate to the circumstances of modern life.

One of those words, *responsibility*, was initially used mostly in context to political leadership and the obligations of a representative government. It wasn't until later in time that it was understood as an individual's moral imperative and the concept of free will. Today, it is even used in a broken-down fashion, as in our ability to respond to a situation. Our ability to respond and our awareness of our response is where I would like to explore the civil grace of responsibility, especially in terms of how we communicate today.

In our modern world, where one can sit behind a device and deliver all sorts of communications, we have so much power at our fingertips. We can share brilliant ideas, and we can also destroy each other. We all know that despite the nursery rhyme we learned, words do hurt often more than actions against us. Words can also be used to misguide us and create chaos where there is none. We have to be mindful of not only what we put out there but also our response-ability to what we take into our minds.

Some analysts believe we are products of a political and media cycle that never stops and too often gives license for us to copy that behavior. Continuously generated sound bites and tweets overrule common sense and courtesy. The phrases "thank you" and "I'm sorry," which used to be expected, are not always present in our connections with each other. Cleverness can be more acceptable than consideration. Wisdom is paved over by expediency. We have to take response-ability for what we consume when it comes to what we see online and in the news, whether or not it is true.

There is an infatuation with the virtual world at a loss of the real world. For example, mobile phones are now accepted as standard at the table and often get in the way of real communication. This is a tug-of-war at my house with the kids. I get rid of the phones, and they still have a watch that connects to everything. Business can be done with a click of the button, and there isn't the chance to develop relationships like there was before.

Real meaning in life isn't about getting the last word or having the most likes. Not to be a buzzkill, but the ending is the same for all of us, give or take a few details. Wouldn't it be wonderful if we were present to each other and treated each other a little better on the journey? The civil grace of responsibility invites us to slow down and consider our ability to respond to one another, to be fully here now.

I once read a line by Emma M. Seppälä that expresses this succinctly: "Our impulse to broadcast our lives makes us miss out on them." After reading that line, I made a conscious decision to curtail my use of social media. I had hundreds of "friends," but when really considering the depth of our relationships, it wasn't the same feeling as when I engaged in person. Research now shows the more time you spend on social media, the unhappier you are. Social media has been such a gift in some ways; my husband and I initially connected with each other that way. But it was the eye-to-eye, face-to-face, arm-in-arm presence that has truly enriched our relationship for the long haul. There are also those things I still have to engage in for my job and to advertise events.

I decided to see for myself whether I could change my response to the world by changing my relationship to social media and the onslaught of data in my life. Some friends were offended by my scaling back, but I assured them that friendship starts in a million connections beyond Facebook or Instagram. We could still do lunch or catch up after work. Waking up to read a good book, meditate, or look outside definitely was a better way to begin my day than grabbing my phone. At times I felt like I was missing out, yet when I brought the phone and social media back, I felt like they were a waste of time. I could do other things with my life. It is a balancing act, but because of the power it evokes and the thrill of getting that like, we have to make sure we are taking the time to unwind from the web.

Remember when we spent more time connecting with cherished friends in person, and when we had to hear the latest news face-to-face or at least by voice over the phone lines? The civil grace of responsibility is about connecting with one another in real life rather than have it be replaced by a virtual world. It means to really be there, not just as if we are all on a stage sharing what we want to share, showing up only halfway and keeping out those things that we wish, but to be real with one another. It means taking response-ability into our relationships with and for each other. This applies to our leaders.

When I spent time in Washington, I met a shopkeeper who had been there for a long time. I asked him, "What do you think has changed this town?" His response will stay with me forever. "They don't sit down together anymore to have dinner. They all rely on tweets and texts. They all want to have the soundbite that gets news coverage."

Psychologists are starting to challenge the effects of social media on the human connection from the earliest ages. The subtle eye contact that happens between parent and child is so critical to mind development, but more and more, we are multitasking to stay on top of it all, and we miss that interaction. Imagine looking into each other's eyes at meals instead of feeling the need to always glance at the phone. Going to places and savoring the experience is much different than getting caught up in the selfie you need to take. Get out from behind the obstacle of the lens and really look. Feel the response in your being.

We achieve more in meetings when we can connect face-to-face because communication is found in the nuances of gesture, reaction, and body language that is lost otherwise. On a more challenging level, the disparaging words we sometimes use with one another when we sit behind a keyboard would seldom cross the lips while sitting face-to-face. Unplugging can be truly liberating.

Though personal connection takes more time and sometimes money to do so, consider the rewards of a happier life. Reconnecting in familiar ways brings us back to each other, gives us new abilities to honestly respond, and can create a unique experience.

The civil grace of responsibility is about showing up. It is about how we choose to show up to the world and whether we are willing to engage, knowing our ideas will have an impact on the receiver. It is about being honest with ourselves and knowing that our friends probably don't just sit around together with a drink. They struggle like we do. Therefore, we can stop beating ourselves up for feeling out of it. We can take advantage of the extra time we aren't online to develop ourselves in meaningful ways. We can pick up the phone to call someone (remember, this is what it used to do) and connect for conversation or to get together.

We are more than our likes and the number of our "friends." It is okay that we don't agree. We don't have to demolish one another to prove our point. Like my mom used to say, "Just because they do that on television, that doesn't make it okay." The same is true of being online. We need to own up to who we are and realize we can be better than what we see represented in the mass media world. We are brilliant beings who are here to illuminate the world.

Reflection

Take a one-week break from the social media you use. If it is helpful, delete the apps or move them off your homepage. Take note of how you feel each day. Are you concerned you are being left out? Do you feel uninformed? Does it bother you at all? Do you feel happier? With all the time you are reclaiming, do something you enjoy.

JUSTICE

Etymology: Latin *justitia*, "righteousness, equity;" from *iustus*, "upright, just, quality of being fair;" Old French *justice*, Old English *iustise*, "administration of the law"

> Each time a man stands up for an ideal, or acts to improve the lot of others, or strikes out against injustice, he sends forth a tiny ripple of hope, and crossing each other from a million different centers of energy and daring, those ripples build a current that can sweep down the mightiest walls of oppression and resistance.
>
> —Robert Kennedy

In light of current events, I have been thinking a lot about the oath that one takes upon entering an office of any nature in America. An oath is a promise and an affirmation: "I give my sincere intention and solemn word." These are the words of the U.S. presidential oath of office:

> Will to the best of my ability, preserve, protect, and defend the Constitution of the United States. So help me God.

So help me God. Interesting, isn't it? Even from the very beginning, we recognize the need to call for that divine inner guidance to help us in our part of this work. As fallible human beings, we definitely cannot do it alone without the wisdom and spirit of grace that comes in the pursuit of justice.

How can we build upon these promises and make sure we are creating a nation and world that works for all? So many vows are broken in these modern days—our pledge to preserve, protect, and defend—but what is it that we are promising? An ideal? A better way of life? Are we promising to each other? Because today, especially in my daily business, no one has faith in another's word unless it is in writing. What do we do with these words that are spoken by the leaders of our great nation when it feels like they are just ... words?

We take them to heart—our own hearts. We have to own our authority.

You don't need an office to make an impact in your nation and promote liberty and justice for all. There are many examples in history of people who decided it was time to step up to the plate. It was their cry for justice that brought us closer to our ideals. But we don't have to wait until we are at the breaking point. Every act, no matter how small, sends ripples that grow.

I nominate every American citizen to take the oath to preserve, protect, and defend the Constitution of the United States every day. Why? Because it is our living document. It is living because we consistently understand the words not just as written but also in the application to the current context. We are standing to defend and bring the civil grace of justice for all of the United States. We cannot continue to imagine that any of us can do it alone.

It is time to realize that being silent in a majority is dangerous when we avoid confronting what we see is harming another or violating the principles of justice in our nation. Why is it that we are okay with over 2 million people being incarcerated in our country? Why is it that we are mostly a nation of immigrants but can't seem to come to terms with a decent immigration policy that allows our doors to be open to the tired, the poor, the huddled masses yearning to breathe free? Why are we okay to sleep at night when millions in our country are homeless, food-insecure, and lack primary medical care?

The civil grace of justice stands on firm ground, demanding that we walk our talk to make a more perfect union. That includes everyone, regardless of race, color, national origin, religion, sex, familial status, disability, as well as sexual orientation and age, among others. When I was running for public office, I reminded my challengers that as a real estate broker, these were the protected class that I must defend in the public's pursuit of housing. How should this be different for any official who seeks to represent the public trust through the vote? We, in an official capacity, must stand for justice for all and mean what we say. Justice is about coming into alignment with one another.

Too many people are talking glibly about uncivil war and calling each other names. This is dangerous talk, and it is stoked by fearmongers who want to bring out the worst in us. As Martin Luther King Jr. wisely said, "Injustice anywhere is a threat to justice everywhere." We have to stop threatening one another with our words and actions.

I call upon every one of us to summon up what Abraham Lincoln called the better angels of our nature. We are the living legacy of the declaration that "all people [my word] are created equal, endowed by their Creator with certain unalienable rights ... life, liberty and the pursuit of happiness." Let that sink in and know that you are part of the manifestation of something bigger. We should not let the fire of Liberty be drowned out by people who have no courage and who think walls and separation are the answer.

After my campaign, I was invited into the classroom with some young students to listen to their concerns. Their teacher said they needed to hear from someone who could answer their questions about what was happening in our country. "What has you worried?" I asked them. The resounding answer among the diverse room: war. They are worried we won't keep our promises. We need to do better to make sure the world is safe and more just for the next generation and beyond. This goes not only to economics and social issues but also to the environment and health.

We can preserve, protect, and defend what is essential for all while making sure those who are the least among us can go to sleep at night knowing they can count on us. It is about civility, but not in the sense that we turn a blind eye or simply mind our manners. It is time to look into the mirror in an examination of our role in the process. The walls of controlling organizations are tumbling down in so many ways because they don't work. Now is the time to build partnerships with each other and the countries around the globe. Life on this planet needs to be sustained for all and not just those who can afford it.

We have to first believe that it is possible and work toward healing the places that are wounded. Because we are collected together by the strands of higher ideals that we are equal with one another, it is time for us to work for justice for all. The civil grace of justice calls each of us to have that epiphany about what we all contribute and where we have work to do.

Reflection

Pick an area where you see injustice happening—anywhere around the world. Ask yourself what part you might be playing in making that happen. Consider how you could make one small act to ripple change and promote justice in the world. This exercise might lead you on a new path, so be ready. Often when we ask for guidance in listening to our inner authority, we are led to a whole new way of seeing the world. That call within you is there for a reason. Get moving!

FORGIVENESS

Etymology: Old English *forgiefan*, "to give, grant, allow, remission of a debt, pardon;" Latin *perdonare*, "to pardon an offense or cease the desire to punish, to completely give"

> Forgiveness is the fragrance that the violet sheds on the heel that has crushed it.
>
> —Mark Twain

No other teacher in my life has been as revealing as the civil grace of forgiveness. As someone who can't sit still and watch life happen, I have experienced what my dad would call "the school of hard knocks" from time to time. I have had moments where anger has gotten the better of me. In the space of fear, despair, and deep woundedness, my pain and frustration have sometimes caused me to lash out at those who caused the injury, those I love, and most commonly at myself.

If you are going to be in the dance of life, no matter how much you plan and try to protect yourself, no matter how much wealth or wisdom you have, no one escapes the lessons that pain and suffering bring. To forgive in the original combination of the term meant to completely give. Oh, how this is one of the most difficult things to do in modern life when we have at our disposal all the facts of why we shouldn't trust anyone or be vulnerable if we can do anything to help it.

We cannot know what it means to love deeply if we haven't experienced indifference. We cannot understand the power of generosity unless we have been without. Music would have no ability to stir our souls if it weren't for silence, and we would never be able to wonder at the majesty of the stars if it weren't for darkness. In the universal dichotomy, all are presently shaping and expanding us for something more significant than where we started. When anger, pain, and fear appear, forgiveness is the gift that leads us back to the land of the living.

The English poet Alexander Pope eloquently wrote, "to err is human, to forgive, divine." Indeed, here is the answer to achieving the ultimate freedom. When the arrows that fly no longer can control you, your being has expanded to the level of the divine. Forgiveness is not about forgetting or excusing. It is about taking away the ability of anyone or anything to hold you captive, and it loosens the power of anger and fear to keep you trapped in a web. It is, as Wayne Dyer related, "giving up the idea of drinking the poison with the hope it will affect the other person."

There was a time when I was ready to be done mourning my losses, and I knew I would be at an event where I would see my opponent. Rather than carry the air of arrogance or indifference, I sought her out and told her I was proud of the work she was doing. In that instant, grace came into me, and the feeling that I truly meant those words surged through me. The sadness immediately was lifted, and I felt so free as we embraced. It may not have meant much to her, but I was, in the words of Martin Luther King Jr., free at last from the past grievances I had been holding.

Oprah Winfrey shared, “Forgiveness is giving up the hope that the past could have been any different.” It is letting go of those bonds so the past cannot hold you hostage any longer. In that instant, I stopped living in the past and decided to put my full energy into creating a life of my dreams.

Forgiveness is one of the civil graces because it is the key that unlocks the door to a limitless life and creates the space for healing among nations, between people, and most important in understanding ourselves. We need forgiveness to continue the dance where life allows all to be meaningful and beautiful. The tyrant leader awakens my heart to take action and do what I can to make a better world. A hurtful word that stings invites me to explore the depths of my soul and what is looking to take flight. A tragedy begs me to give of myself for another and to expand so that killing and devastation don’t have the final word.

In the end, forgiveness is the ultimate expression of love. We lift up our spirits so they can freely live and discover the adventures we were meant to take. It allows what I call the “manure moments” to fertilize the seeds of something new to sprout.

Before we enter each new day or each new adventure, it is an opportune time to let go of some baggage. Where are we each being called to forgive? Where do we need to offer an apology for missing the mark? This is a time of awakened energy; the time for business as usual is over. Take the first step on the path to forgiveness and welcome freedom and expansion of your spirit.

Reflection

Search your spirit for something or someone you need to forgive. Without belaboring it, swiftly give yourself the gift of forgiveness. Release whatever it is, whomever it is, and then revel in the freedom that is released.

INSPIRATION

Etymology: Latin from *in* + *spirare*, "to breathe, blow into, breathe upon, excite, inflame;" in Old French *inspiracion*, "inhaling, breathing in, inspiration;" In Middle English "breathe or put life or spirit into the human body as in the sense of divine guidance or inspiration; drawing air into the lungs as inhaling"

> And now here is my secret, a very simple secret: It is only with the heart that one can see rightly; what is essential is invisible to the eye.
>
> —Antoine de Saint-Exupéry

What would it mean if we couldn't breathe? Often when I am talking about what is essential to a group of leaders, I have everyone take a deep breath and hold it. The room starts to get anxious the longer we go, and at once, I ask them, "so what is important to you now?" It typically isn't about success, money, or future goals. The essential thing at that moment is to take a breath.

As I reread this manuscript completed earlier this year, the words "I can't breathe" have powerful meaning beyond what any of us could have imagined. They are the words we will forever remember as those spoken by George Floyd at his wrongful death and the representation of so many people of color who have lost their lives unjustly. They are also the words of hundreds of thousands of people who have died from the coronavirus pandemic, a virus that primarily attacked the lungs and the ability to breathe. These words strike us to the core of life. We all need breath to live, and more than that, we need to take inspired action to preserve that life force for all people. This single act of not being able to take a breath has awakened us to the injustices in our world, especially for people of color. I remember the fearful feeling of having the wind knocked out of me; as a kid, I panicked, trying to remember how to inhale. Lately, as I witness the violence and continued aggression, I start to feel that same panic. What can any of us do to turn the tide toward a more inspired future for all?

The root of the word *inspire* means to breathe. It also means to excite and lift up. What would it mean to live without inspiration? I believe that is when our spirit or our inner fire fades, and life ceases to have a purpose. Our world stops to have a purpose. The wind gets knocked out of us, despair moves in, and the light goes out. During these past few days, I have been listening to stories of the lives of those who are hurting. Each person wants to be heard. Each one is asking us to see one another as true equals. Our nation and the world need deep healing. Through the inspired actions of listening, learning, and loving, we can transform the world. We can understand what needs to happen in our responses to make that more perfect union work for all.

The word *inspiration* also relates the term to "divine guidance." To some traditions, human origin mystically can be traced to the book of Genesis, when the spirit of life was breathed into form. To be inspired is to be filled with life and have breath for the journey. I believe living an inspired life is an essential civil grace that allows us to see beyond our current situation to the horizons of what we are called to be. It links us to the idea that we are all both human and divine beings in this world. It is the call that we have to wake up to amend our ways, atone for the wrongs, and act to bring a better world for all.

Inspiration moves us to expect the best from each other, to challenge, and to care about each other. It allows us to embrace the possible, be awakened, and transcend. We need to seek inspiration to find the way to the common ground that unites us all.

The foundational documents of our democracy were inspired by ideas that we could build a new world and a new way of governing together. We agreed to work for the betterment of all humanity without putting our power into something above us. The application at the time was deeply flawed with slavery and not all being equal. Women and people of color were excluded from the equation, violations to indigenous people deprived them of their land and lives, and discrimination throughout our history has been present. Over time we have made strides to change that. Still, there is growing momentum today that we cannot ignore the continued violence and injustice perpetrated by a systemic belief in domination and control. There has been a global shift, a conscious awakening of the realization (to make real) the ideals of a world that works for all through partnership. One of my hopes is to increase awareness of the importance of citizens working together. Now is the time to ensure all are equal in our daily actions, our laws, and our systems of justice. Most importantly, we have to examine our hearts and see how we can serve this higher purpose.

When we feel discouraged, we can take hope that inspiration will arise if we continue to ask profound questions about our existence and take creative action with our lives. It is "We the People" who have to do the work. In the words of civil rights leader Malcolm X, "When 'I' is replaced with 'we' even illness becomes wellness." We need the ideas of all of us.

My husband, Vince, and I were inspired last year to start a community organization called the Little Barn of Big Ideas on our farm. We wanted to create a space where people can come together and brainstorm about the big ideas in our community and how we can use our talents, build resources, and make a positive impact in areas where we are passionate. We believe that we are not a divided nation; we are diverse, and that gift is going to be the key to changing our country's current climate and our world.

We believe the world's issues will be solved by people coming together to create the changes we seek. Every one of us has a purpose to reveal the creative genius we each carry. Our goal is to create the space for inspiration, engagement, and uplifting of the human spirit so people will launch their purpose into the world. It has been exciting to see our community light up from the idea that we can use what we have to make things better. We don't have to wait for something outside of ourselves.

We are living in extraordinary times right now! We have so many opportunities and possibilities to be inspired. The communication revolution has changed how we can connect, and the speed of sharing ideas is beyond what we could have imagined just a decade ago. It truly is brilliant as much as it is overwhelming! The use of these tools carries an enormous responsibility, but there never has been a time so ripe for the human spirit to transform.

Right now, the world feels pretty unsure and unsafe for too many. Yet there is always room for hope that inside us are the seeds of change for the better. E. B. White, author of one of my favorite childhood books, *Charlotte's Web,* wrote to a despairing young man in the world. He shared, "As long as there is one upright man, as long as there is one compassionate woman, the contagion may spread, and the scene is not desolate ... Hang on to your hat. Hang on to your hope. And wind the clock, for tomorrow is another day."

The civil grace of inspiration reminds us to remember what is essential in life. It calls us to receive the spirit of the wonders of it all. Allow yourself to see the possibilities despite the challenges that may crowd your mind. Look for the ways to open your imagination to manifest a more just, peaceful, and abundant world for all. Anything is possible when you hold the civil grace of inspiration.

Reflection

What is the big idea that inspires you? Is there something you always knew was possible, or a better way to make something happen? Write it down and take an inspired leap toward it every day. Take inspired actions for a more just world. Know in your heart that for such as time as this you were born.

To learn more about what we are doing at the Little Barn of Big Ideas, please visit https://littlebarnofbigideas.com.

COMPASSION

Etymology: French *compassion*, "sympathy, pity, feeling of sorrow or pity caused by the sufferings or misfortunes of another;" Latin *compassionem*, "sympathy;" *compati*, "to suffer together"

> Life is short, and we have never too much time for gladdening the hearts of those who are traveling the dark journey with us. Oh, be swift to love, make haste to be kind.
>
> —Henri Frederic Amiel

American songwriter and musical artist Burt Bacharach said it best: "What the world needs now is love, sweet love. It's the only thing that there's just too little of." The world cannot survive if we refuse to recognize our common bond with one another. The civil grace of compassion is about acknowledging not only our shared humanity but also our connection with all living beings on the planet. This includes loving and having compassion for yourself.

Right now, our world is going through significant transitions, and most of us feel it. We have to remember deep down who we really are. We come from many backgrounds and experiences. We are people who sometimes have to agree to disagree and move forward despite our differences. “We must learn to regard people less in the light of what they do or omit to do, and more in the light of what they suffer,” Dietrich Bonhoeffer wrote while in a Nazi prison. He understood that freedom was possible only in relationship with each other. We all have the common bonds of suffering, and we all have the universal need for compassion.

Finding a way to bring people together in this highly digital age is not easy. It is much safer to stay at home behind your computer and connect only with those whom you like; similarly, it is easier to call others out when you aren’t looking into their eyes. We are in incredibly challenging times due to the growth of what is termed tribalism, but it is also an incredibly exciting time because people are taking action to bring issues from the darkness into the light. We are being called to invoke the spirit of the St. Francis of Assisi prayer, where we seek to understand not just to be understood.

Creating spaces where it is safe to dialogue and debate the more significant issues of our time is essential to our communities and our country. Our founding principles allowed us to sort things out; sometimes we did this better than others. “Our task must be to free ourselves … by widening our circle of compassion to embrace all living creatures and the whole of nature, and it’s beauty,” wrote Albert Einstein.

We can transform our lives and our world if we are willing to make space for the dialogues that we most fear. I saw this in my work on the campaign trail: human-to-human conversations can break down walls, and new ideas and solutions can come forth. Thomas Jefferson shared this notion when he wrote, "The last hope of human liberty in this world rests on us. We ought, for so dear a stake, to sacrifice every attachment and every enmity." The civil grace of compassion invites us to tear down the walls and build bridges to one another to find that common ground.

Leo Buscaglia was one of my favorite teachers on how to have love and compassion. He would say, "Too often we underestimate the power of a touch, a smile, a kind word, a listening ear, an honest compliment, or the smallest act of caring, all of which have the potential to turn a life around." We have that power in these incredible times.

Consider this: if it weren't for all this tension in our society, would any of us be moved to do what we are doing to address these issues? The real challenges we all face are the catalysts for the growth that is happening. The very fact that we still see behaviors as unreal means that we know what is real. "The true crisis of civility is if none of us cared. If we all stopped caring about what counts as appropriate behavior, then civility's not in crisis, it's dead," shared Keith Bybee, author of *How Civility Works*. When we see unbelievable actions displayed, that means we recognize what we do believe, and from this heart of compassion, we can create communities that work for all.

We live in the paradox of being individuals who need a community to survive. Sometimes we hyper-inflate the idea of personal power in our culture because we value individual success as the ultimate goal. This belief can lead to the overwhelming feeling of having to make it on your own, but it also disconnects us from each other. However, consider a day in your life. The actions of so many people and elements make it possible. From our earliest days, someone or something was there to support our next step. Peter Block's *Community: The Structure of Belonging*, discusses how this shift in viewing the world shapes building an alternative future. "The essential challenge is to transform the isolation and self-interest within our communities into connectedness and caring for the whole." We need both individual efforts and collective efforts. None of us can do it alone.

Nature once again has a great example of teaching us how we can do this. We have beehives on our farm and have read extensively to understand how to keep the hives thriving. I am fascinated by the magic of making honey. In his book, *Honeybee Democracy*, Thomas Seeley explores these majestic colonies of insects who collectively work for the survival of the hive. Despite the myth of the "queen bee" ruling the rest, each bee has a unique role, and the success of the colony is tied together in democratic debate and organizing with each other. Individual bees with mutual respect and shared interests secure the well-being of all. Besides, those little insects make possible the food on our plates. We depend on them, and they rely on us to make wise choices with our environment. All of life is a web, and one ripple affects the whole.

The civil graces are more than manners. They are principles that address the question of how we shall live with one another and find a way to a life of meaning and purpose. It is about understanding that each of us will have a different perspective, but we will not make it if we think we can go it alone.

When we choose to see the world as falling apart, there is plenty out there to suggest we are right. However, if you wish to view these changing times as an opportunity for us to confront some age-old behaviors and beliefs that no longer fit, then there is definitely a reason for hope. The challenge of our modern world with so much exhausting noise surrounding us is to do some introspection. In the epic tale of the clash between opposites, *Moby Dick,* Herman Melville points to the value of opposing views. "To enjoy bodily warmth, some small part of you must be cold, for there is no quality in this world that is not what it is merely by contrast. Nothing exists in itself." We need each other to help wrestle with opposites to find the truths.

The tone of our national politics is probably an area where we have limited control, but we can control the way we speak, post, and comment on those issues. I read an article in the newspaper the other day that had me infuriated, and upon doing a little more research, I found out that there was another side to the story. It made me think twice about posting my opinions. How often is there another side of the story that doesn't always come immediately to light? Why spend time justifying my actions because someone was worse? Isn't it much easier to look outside and point to one another than to do the inner work of transformation? We all know what we can do differently if we are willing to be honest with ourselves. How can we be the change we wish for the world?

The reason I am hopeful about this current era is that many people are asking these questions and are engaging in meaningful dialogue. They are seeking to learn how to have civil discourse, and individuals on opposing sides realize that something has to be done to bring the whole back together. Issues that were long in the shadows are coming to the public square to be examined. Compassion is the invitation to go deeper to understand one another. We are invited to open our minds to new connections and new relationships to see what magic happens there!

Reflection

Look at your circle of friends and see how you are doing with creating diversity in your life. Do you choose friends only with whom you agree and have similar values? Do you seek out opportunities to listen to other viewpoints without the need to judge? Of all that occupies our time and space on this earth, the most important things end up being the relationships we keep. In the spirit of compassion, try to expand your circle.

INTEGRITY

Etymology: Old French *integrité*, “innocence, blamelessness, chastity, purity;” Latin *integritatem*, “soundness, wholeness, completeness”

> The moment we begin to fear the opinions of others and hesitate to tell the truth that is in us, and from motives of policy are silent when we should speak, the divine floods of light and life no longer flow into our souls. Every truth we see is ours to give the world, not to keep for ourselves alone, for in so doing we cheat humanity out of their rights and check our own development.
>
> —Elizabeth Cady Stanton

When I was a child, I was taught to never lie even with small things. If you did, you would have to tell a bigger lie to cover that up. Eventually, you would wind up so far from the truth that you might not find your way back. That was when someone’s word was as good as gold, and those who didn’t keep their word were disadvantaged in business and social circles. It was a thing everyone knew, and those individuals weren’t trusted.

The world is very different today in some respects; with video cameras all over the place, people can get caught saying one thing and then quite the opposite moments later. Our words have lost their value, especially in the realms of telling the truth. Does the soul grow numb after a while when it is hidden in lies, coated like a scaly covering that can no longer feel?

I like to think that most people tell the truth or want to tell the truth, but maybe they are only telling what they want to believe. I wanted to serve in public office my whole life but could never grow comfortable with the idea that to succeed in that world, I would have to make compromises with my values. I guess I have to thank my lucky stars that things happened the way they did, and I can still look myself in the eye knowing the truth of my being.

There are times when integrity is hard. There is so much data available at our fingertips, but we always have to question the motive behind who is sharing the information. What if I support someone and then discover parts of that person that go against what I believe? Do I discount the person entirely or justify that we are all human beings who fail? During my brother's divinity studies, he learned that the term *sin* came from archery. When your arrow misses the mark, they would call out, "Sin!" Integrity calls us to own up when we miss the mark in our lives—not to flog ourselves, but to take better aim next time.

Words and actions matter. Those in power do need to be held accountable for their words. As one of my college professors, Dr. McAnaw, would say, "You have to be able to speak truth to power!" I think that is our charge in this modern day: to speak the truth and make sure that those who want to represent us do the same. How can we do this? In many ways. By the way you spend your money. Are you paying attention to where you invest, where you shop, and the organizations you support? Do you really pay attention to how you vote with your money? As I campaigned, I learned the unfortunate truth that organizations that seemed to be amazing actually missed the mark in delivering what they promised on the surface.

Corporations and outside influences support candidates simply to get favorable laws passed. It is all about power, and these interests very often supersede the people who should be represented. Why is it that America, the land that used to lead in solving problems, is so slow to resolving anything? Follow the money, and you will find the truth.

When asked what kind of government we shall have, Benjamin Franklin responded, "A republic, if you can keep it." In a republic, the people are the sovereigns, and the truth is we have to start acting like it and pay attention to the actions of those who represent us. Think about what you read. Consider the source. Entertain opposing views if you can, if only to learn something different. Get involved in the process and write letters to the editor, to your representatives, and to your president. Ask questions. Then maybe we will get closer to the truth.

Reflection

For one day, follow your words and your actions. Do they match up to what you believe or what you say you believe? We all know when we are off balance, and this isn't a tattletale, but call yourself out. Realign. Then see how you feel moving forward in your newfound wholeness.

VULNERABILITY

Etymology: From Latin *vulnerabilis*, "wounding;" or *vulnerare*, "to wound, hurt, injure, maim;" from *vulnus*, "wound, pluck, to tear, susceptible to attack, harm, or exposure"

> Everything in nature is given some form of resilience by which it can rehearse finding its way, so that, when it does, it is practiced and ready to seize its moment. This includes us. When things don't work out—when loves unexpectedly end or careers stop unfolding—it can be painful and sad, but refusing this larger picture keeps us from finding our resilience.
>
> —Mark Nepo

Years ago, I was a research assistant to poet and author Mark Nepo on his work *The Book of Awakening.* We had many fascinating conversations with our team, but the one I will always remember was about salmon. On its pilgrimage to lay its eggs, the salmon's ability to fly upstream relies on the salmon turning its soft underside to meet the pounding surf. By opening the most vulnerable part of its being, it ascends along the journey. This image Mark shared has helped me open to my core purpose and ideas, even when it may have been risky or painful to do so. As the salmon are called to return up the waterfall, we are called to open ourselves to the truth of our being.

This can feel incredibly vulnerable, especially in our modern age, when we may be quickly exposed in ways we hadn't imagined. After my campaign, I felt as low as I ever remember being and wanted to escape from the world. I had given it my all, but it wasn't enough. I was worn out and felt I had let down everyone. My family depended on me, so I had to get back to work and put myself back into the arena.

Over the past several months, things have emerged to push me a little further. I saw the need for spaces like I had in my early career to talk about the things that matter. My big idea of running was crushed, and I know the pain of that. However, I could use that energy, my most vulnerable moment, to push me to a place where I could help others bring forth their big ideas and together solve the issues that we face as a community and a world.

Brené Brown speaks of vulnerability as "having the courage to show up and be seen when we have no control over the outcome." We like to calculate our chances, so vulnerability feels uncomfortable, ironically like being a fish out of water. Vulnerability steps into the dance of life and takes the lead when most of the time, we would rather hideout on the sidelines. Vulnerability happens when we take the risk to get close to another, to hear another side of the debate, to watch the one you love to go through a challenge and feel helpless about what to do. We don't like this feeling and will very often run in the opposite direction.

Not being able to "fix" or find a solution for yourself or the ones you care about is incredibly difficult. Friends with the best intentions wanting you to get over it and go back to the way you were before can cause you to withdraw and become outraged at the situation. We can't push the river. Sometimes when you have waves crashing around your head, it is time to swim deeper to where the water is still. We have to let time heal the wounds. This can be exceptionally difficult if you thought you had it altogether or were in control. Sometimes the best place to go is on your knees, to be vulnerable, and to ask for guidance.

I once read of an account of a father's grief for the unexpected loss of his son that genuinely touched my soul and opened the floodgates so I could let go of the shame I was holding inside. He wrote, "At one point in history, mankind believed the world was a flat table, and those foolhardy enough to venture too near the edge would fall off into a terrible world of fierce sea monsters and destruction upon the rocks." We no longer believe that, but often we fear to venture out and being exposed or destroyed. When you are feeling vulnerable, we can beat ourselves up for taking risks and failure. We have to be willing to give ourselves a lifeline and make peace with our pure human nature in all its fabulousness and fragility. Sometimes we don't know how to get back out, and we need mentors and good books to hold our hands until we are ready to return.

Fear is never a good place to start. We have to let go of what would have been to give space to what is meant to be. I began to have meetings around the big table in the barn, and we came up with an idea: the Little Barn of Big Ideas. It is a space to give birth to dreams and big ideas while making room for everyone at the table—precisely what I wanted to do when I was in Congress. Having a place for the genius in all of us to emerge while having supportive mentors around the table is liberating, and it feels a little less vulnerable. Our dream is to continue to grow a bigger vision at our table in our little barn.

Vulnerability is a civil grace as reminder that our nation was built by people who took risks to create something different than the status quo. Our world has been continually redefined by individuals who stood up and spoke out about their dreams and ideas. Our world still depends on this energy to come forth from each of us. We cannot let fear stop us from moving forward when we know our spirit is being called higher. Vulnerability is a part of being human and is the gateway of our connection to one another. It is in those tender spaces where we can heal and overcome. We have to be willing to take the leap and throw all that we are into the forces that will carry us to the next level. We go to the place where we give birth to something greater within us.

Reflection

Rising through my own vulnerability gave birth to a new role: to be a mother of possibility. I want to know: What is your big idea? I hope you will share that when you are ready with the world. We need your big ideas!

PATIENCE

Etymology: From the Latin verb *pati* "to suffer;" same root of the word "passion;" French and Middle English *pacience*, "quality of being willing to bear adversities, calm endurance of misfortune, suffering;" used of persons as well as of navigable rivers

> Have Patience with everything that remains unsolved in your heart. Try to love the questions themselves, like locked rooms and like books written in a foreign language. Do not now look for the answers. They cannot now be given to you because you could not live them. It is a question of experiencing everything. At present you need to live the question.
>
> —Rainer Maria Rilke

"Patience is a virtue." Unfortunately, it is one of which I have little tolerance. Getting slowed down by indecision, lack of action, or things not moving quickly enough can wear me down like nothing else. I often say things like, "Make it happen!" "There's no time like the present!" "Move!" and "C'mon!" You can almost imagine me as one of those parents who was very animated in the bleachers as the kids played their sports. If you were there, I apologize!

The wise sage Lao Tzu stated, “Nature does not hurry, yet everything is accomplished.” My favorite memory of how this is so was the anticipation of my first child. When I was first married, there was a chance that we couldn’t have kids. Having a family was something I’d always dreamed of, and I remember making the decision that I would find a way; after all, my mom had twelve kids. I figured the odds were I could do the same. Things didn’t go as I had hoped, and each month I would be crushed that nothing was happening. Most people would say, “You have to be patient. Let nature take its course.” Whatever. Frustrated, I got involved in my work at the time, which was digging deeper into freedom and human rights and how we could make humanity act a little kinder to one another.

My research took me to other countries, and I had an excellent guide to take me around and be my translator. I remember riding in a taxi toward the next village one day. I commented on a large white bird sitting on top of a house as we passed. The taxi driver turned and said something to my guide, Sophie, and she said, “He told me to tell you are probably pregnant because you just saw a stork.” We both laughed at that comment and continued our journey.

During the trip, there were unexpected limitations on where we could go because the timing happened to coincide with when world leaders were there for other reasons. We couldn’t enter when they were there because of security and had to redirect a lot of our trip. I didn’t get everywhere I needed to go, but we saw enough places to get an understanding of the evil that happened there. For some reason, I was not to see it all.

Upon returning back from my trip, I discovered I was expecting. I could hardly believe it, but it was true. We enrolled in classes, read everything we could find, and measured my food to make sure everything would be perfect. We thought we were prepared and in control. It was not an easy pregnancy; she was breached until the very last minute, and her delivery was exceptionally long because I was trying very hard to bring her in naturally. My patience was tried at every turn, and my body wasn't cooperating. I had to let go of the ideal I held in my mind in order to safely bring her forth. She arrived days later, thankfully healthy and strong. We decided to name her Abigail, which means "God's laughter." God had the last laugh despite what was believed.

In a way, I think her spirit from the beginning kept me from witnessing even greater horrors than I saw on my trip. The profound sorrow would possibly have affected her beyond what I carried. She was coming on her own terms. Today, Abby is a young woman who is determined to make good things happen in the world. I had to be patient for her and then for Kate and Jack, who arrived in the years that followed. They had their own schedules then and now. Someone once shared about children, "As in the beginning, so as in the middle, so as in the end." They each arrived with a personality and spirit of their own that has continued throughout the years. The three of them are wondrous gifts, have been my best teachers, and are my inspiration to work for a better world.

In connection with being a mom, I have learned that if we cannot learn to work with the rhythms of life, our impatience creates additional stress, pain, and ultimately conflict in a world that needs more love and understanding. Patience is required to hear the questions instead of rushing to find the answers. Sometimes in our haste, we overlook what is obvious or what is trying to help us. We miss the idiosyncrasies that could hold the key to our discovery. We make things harder when we simply have to wait and find the pulse. It isn't time yet. Elements aren't aligned, and what we don't know could harm us beyond what is necessary.

I think a lot of the cruelty that has happened in our world comes from individuals who believed in fear and lack. They convinced and pressured others to buy into that false narrative.

Although there are sometimes many reasons to despair in the way things are, and we feel powerless to stop them, the civil grace of patience asks us to endure and live the questions to find the deeper truths because that is where the solutions are. This can be extraordinarily difficult when we witness tragedy or violation of humankind. It is absolutely not to be silent, but to be open to receiving what is trying to come forth so we may put our actions and voices toward meaningful resolution. Rather than shout from the energy of more fear, we are called to find the strength that comes from authentic engagement and alignment with what is real.

In her amazing book, *The Soul of Money,* Lynne Twist describes "the job of our time is to hospice the death of the old unsustainable systems and structures and to midwife the birth of new sustainable systems and new ways of being." We are called to come with love and compassion to create a world that works together in partnership and collaboration. This process will require our wisdom and patience.

After my trip, I dreamed for many weeks about it. It was as if the spirits I encountered needed to share their experiences so I could facilitate a deeper understanding of what we must do to make sure these violations never happen again. The stories of courageous individuals who acted from such love for others stick with me. I will forever hold the space and honor their memory. To endure, to undergo, to experience what life unravels and somehow find a way to make meaning takes patience and a willingness to listen. Yet it is precisely what is needed today when we witness what is happening in our world.

Patience is not about ignoring or to rest on our laurels, thinking it is someone else's problem. It is about taking right action and working with the rhythms that are connected to the whole of life. It is about not adding to the fire but bringing the elements that will put out the fire completely. It is about navigating the best way to heal the situation and bring justice.

I put off writing this chapter because I am still learning how to work with patience. To me, it always seems like a weak stance because isn't it more powerful to just do something about a situation? The older I get (and hopefully wiser), I am learning that often the first thing that comes to my mind is not what is needed. It is coming from a less than whole space ... usually, it is coming from fear.

"What will happen if I don't say anything?" Or, "I've got to do something about it!" Relationships with those closest to me are when this is most challenging. There have been times when I have said or done things in haste only to wish I could take them back. Instead of solving anything, I became part of the problem.

Statesman and philosopher Sir Edmund Burke said, "Our Patience will achieve more than our force." In our current reality where ideas are quickly shared, we need the civil grace of patience to remind us that we can make things happen, but just as the flower emerges in time from the bud and the chick finds its way out of the shell, we have to align with the rhythms of life. We need to listen to the still, small questions inside us and pray that we have the good sense to know what to do when we are summoned.

Reflection

Get quiet, away from any distractions or noise. Listen for that small voice inside you. If you haven't checked in for a while, it can take time to hear it. Be patient. Listen for the rhythms within you that are calling you to be a part of the whole of life. Explore the things that cause you unrest. Ask for guidance from the voice within to help you to know when and how to act.

PERSEVERANCE

Etymology: Old French *perseverance*, "persistence, endurance;" Latin *per* + *serverus*, "very serious;" *perseverantia*, "steadfastness, constancy"

> Once we believe in ourselves, we can risk curiosity, wonder, spontaneous delight, or any experience that reveals the human spirit.
>
> —e. e. cummings

Isn't it interesting, the things we choose to remember in our lives? For instance, one of my earliest memories of school was in kindergarten, happily coloring away with a green crayon only to look up and realize everyone else had followed the direction and used red. The teacher scolded me for not doing as the others had. When I think of it now, I chuckle. There has always been a little "color outside the box" in my nature. At the time, I felt diminished, as if I'd failed. Even though years later, I went on to graduate at the top of my class, that idea stuck with me.

I grew up in a large family, and we were always trying to measure up to the older siblings. It was as if your very survival depended on differentiation and achievement. My perseverance developed in each accomplishment, and thus I dreamed big dreams. The belief that I could become anything I put my heart and mind to was a core component of that drive. Each of us has that natural gift of wonder and having a trusting space to step out is essential to reveal our purpose.

One of the challenges of our time is the institutions we were taught to trust are undergoing a metamorphosis, and this energy can create a lot of insecurity in each of us. We aren't sure whether we can believe someone's word, in the organizations that use to be the backbone of society, or in our self-knowing. Are we getting the full story? Where is the information coming from that we read? What's the motive? Who is behind any agenda? We are afraid to speak out because of what might happen next. Why step out of line and be called out? We are inundated with information and not quite sure what is fact and what is fiction. In a world of questions, the civil grace of perseverance is what can give us hope that we can rise above it all no matter what it is, as long as we put our minds to it.

There is a concept that seems to be gaining popularity, and I think it is timely. The word is grit. Grit is when you have the passion and perseverance for the long road ahead to achieve your goals. It is the fire inside the one who isn't afraid to sweat it out in the trenches because there is something deeper at stake. It is the characteristic we love in our movies: when everything seems to be going wrong, the heroine keeps going to victory.

You may have seen Simon Sinek, the world-renowned author of *Start with Why.* His TED Talk was about how "people don't care what you do; they care why you do it." I love his work, and it has inspired me to really consider why

I take on the tasks I do in life. It is an essential question we have to ask. Sometimes, though, we can ponder this question and get analysis paralysis, where we forever philosophize and brainstorm but have no action. There comes a time when you simply have another question: Why not? Why not you? Why not now?

We have every resource in this country to make things happen, including brilliant people, money, natural resources, ideas, and the freedom to do it. We could solve every significant crisis and issue. The problem is that the emphasis is on the wrong thing. The focus is on the money and not the people. Why is this a problem? Because it isn't always just about the economy. It is about making a world where all can thrive. Because in our political process, when candidates have to bend every which way to raise funds to feed the consultants recommended by the leadership ecosystem, they fill their pockets full of dollars, which equals promises to those who put them there.

If those dollars come from special interests and corporations, they want a return on their investment. Those "contributions" equate to influence and votes, which is why we don't see sensible legislation in almost any area. Think about it: we are the wealthiest nation in the world. We have the resources to have the best education, health care, quality of life, inventions, and economy, but instead we have a process that pits one side against another, all in the name of winning. Who loses? The American people do—all of us.

This is a very disappointing story so far, if we are considering what we can do. Why have any hope at all? I will tell you why. We the people are the actual power in this country. We have lost sight of that fact because the emphasis is on dividing us. We have forgotten that we can make a change in our country when things aren't working. Our elected officials are supposed to hold this power in trust with us. It is okay to color outside the box and try new things. Innovation is at our core! We are living through a historical moment, and persevering together will be critical.

Perseverance comes from the Latin word *perseverantia*, which means steadfastness and constancy. When we hold steadfast to the ideals that connect us, we find our truth and our hope again. Perseverance is a civil grace because it is those self-evident truths that form the foundation of our nation and our individual lives. It is the belief that all are created equal and have gifts to bring forth to make a more perfect union. We have to take the energy we are placing in fighting for dying institutions, and we must focus that energy on the core of what made this nation so incredible: the belief that the people have the power to self-govern and the ability to dream new dreams.

One theme I repeat several times in this book because it is so essential is the idea that we are not divided; we are diverse. It is this diversity that gives us all the options to find the solutions to the questions we are asking. It is with continuing to stand with each other that we will change the world for the better. From my perspective, there is no one in the world committed to your ideas, dreams, and hopes like you are. Uncovering your purpose is why you are here. If we are waiting for someone outside ourselves to solve our issues or to find our answers, it is never going to happen. Bluntly, I was in the belly of the beast, and if it is going to happen, we are going to have to find a way to make it happen. Waiting around for someone to be our (s)hero is over.

Recently, I came across a line of poetry that read, "what didn't you do to bury me/but you forgot that I was a seed." The pressures we feel in our world today are there for a reason. Each of us is being asked to look again and see how we can bring forth our genius. What's your big idea? Every one of us has something to offer, and it is why my husband and I created the space for everyone to bring forth their big ideas and help them grow. It is up to each of us to think differently than what we are always being told. The most powerful thing we can do is to ask questions and listen to one another. We must not buy into this notion that we are against one another—*we are stronger together.*

The lessons of life don't always make sense immediately. It takes time for the path to reveal itself. Each of us has had moments that shaped our view of the world. Your story and your ideas are needed more than ever. I invite you to consider the civil grace of perseverance to be your companion on the journey so you may rekindle your curiosity, hope in your abilities, belief in a better world, and willingness to work with all of us to make it happen.

I wrote this book because I wanted to tell my story in the hopes it will inspire you to get up and live your fullest life. All I wanted to do my whole life was fix the issues that had the world concerned. Guess what? The world doesn't want to be fixed. It took a political two-by-four to help me realize that. The circus of our national political scene is just that: people parading around and promising to be the answer to all your problems. I have discovered you cannot drain the swamp; you can only find a way to redirect the water to be a resource. You cannot solve others' problems until they are ready to accept your help. The most important thing is to play your song, write your book, or start your movement, if only for that spirit within you that must be expressed in this lifetime.

While I write this book, I am still wrestling with my political bug, as I call it. Like a kid who burns her hand on the hot stove but never learns, I get swept up in the political drama each time. Every time my hand gets burned, I swear that is the last time. I care so deeply about this American experience—the good, the bad, the struggles, and the beautiful moments. I hope I live long enough to see a woman president, true equality for all, to see us eradicate poverty and major illness. I hope we can help each other manifest our destiny so that we all can enjoy those self-evident truths: life, liberty, and the pursuit of happiness.

Reflection

Write down your dream. Answer the question, "Why not?" in terms of why not you and why not now. Print those words or create an image. Put it somewhere that you will see each day as a reminder that you are here to do something. Send me a note at civilgraces@gmail.com or visit us online at littlebarnofbigideas.com if you need a word of encouragement and to let me know how it is going. Let's do this together!

WHAT ARE YOUR CIVIL GRACES?

Please add them to the pages that follow. I love the poem "Wild Geese" by Mary Oliver and encourage you to read it in its entirety. It has been a great comfort to me as I get back out in the world to share my ideas. The lines below are summoning all of us. No matter who we are, what we carry, or where we are in our lives, we each need to bring our gifts to join in the creation of this great circle of life.

> Whoever you are, no matter how lonely,
> the world offers itself to your imagination,
> calls to you like the wild geese, harsh and exciting—
> over and over announcing your place
> in the family of things.

Civil Graces Continued ...

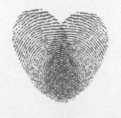

ACKNOWLEDGMENTS

I have had so many teachers over the years, and I am grateful to all of them. They have inspired me to explore the deeper questions.

This year, on the 100th Anniversary of the ratification of the 19th Amendment, I want to honor all the suffragists and suffragettes who sacrificed their lives and made it their mission that women could vote and have the opportunity to run for political office. We must show up every time to vote and uphold their legacy.

I could never have survived the journey that led to this book or completed it without the love and courageous support of my husband, Bernard Vincent Moro, Jr. I am amazingly blessed by my three children, Abby, Kate, and Jack, as well as by my two stepchildren, Rachel and Vinnie. They all inspire me to keep working for a better world!

If you are interested in the etymology of words like me, there are many excellent resources online that you can check out. It is incredible to look at the origins of words and connect to their deeper meanings.

What follows is a listing of sources I used in this book, but there are so many more to share! Please follow the Civil Graces Project online at www.civilgraces.com. Much love to you!

Elizabeth Moro

SOURCES

Amiel, Henri Frédéric. *Amiel's Journal.* Gloucester: Dodo Press, 2006.

Andrews, Andy. *The Butterfly Effect.* Nashville: Thomas Nelson Publishers, 2010.

Bacharach, Burt, and Hal David. "What the World Needs Now Is Love." 1965.

Beattie, Melody. *Codependent No More: How to Stop Controlling Others and Start Caring for Yourself.* Center City, MN: Hazelden Publishing, 1986.

Block, Peter. *Community: The Structure of Belonging.* Oakland, CA: Berrett-Koehler Publishers, Inc., 2008.

Bonhoeffer, Dietrich. *Letters and Papers from Prison.* New York: Touchstone Books, 1997.

BrainyMedia Inc. "Madeleine Albright Quotes." Accessed March 6, 2020, https://www.brainyquote.com/quotes/madeleine_albright_432623.

Brown, Brené. *Daring Greatly: How the Courage to Be Vulnerable Transforms the Way We Live, Love, Parent, and Lead.* New York: Avery Publishing, 2015.

Burke, Edmund, and L. G. Mitchell. *Reflections on the Revolution in France.* Oxford: Oxford University Press, 1999.

Buscaglia, Leo. *Love.* Thorofare, NJ: Slack, Incorporated, 1972.

Bybee, Keith. *How Civility Works.* Palo Alto, CA: Stanford University Press, 2016.

Capra, Frank. *It's a Wonderful Life,* Liberty Films, Inc., 1947.

Christianopoulos, Dino. *The Body and the Wormwood.* Translated by Nicholas Kostis. Athens: Odysseas Publications, 1995.

Cummings, E. E. *100 Selected Poems.* New York: Grove Press, 1994.

Dass, Ram, and Mirabai Bush. *Walking Each Other Home: Conversations on Loving and Dying.* Boulder, CO: Sounds True, 2018.

deBeauvoir, Simone. *All Men Are Mortal.* New York: World Publishing, 1955.

Dyer, Wayne. *21 Days to Master Success and Inner Peace.* Carlsbad, CA: Hay House, 2012.

Dyer, Wayne. *Change Your Thoughts, Change Your Life: Living the Wisdom of the Tao.* Carlsbad, CA: Hay House, 2006.

Dyer, Wayne W. *Living the Wisdom of the Tao.* Carlsbad, CA: Hay House, 2008.

Dyer, Wayne W. *The Shift.* Carlsbad, CA: Hay House, 2012.

Eisler, Riane. *The Chalice & The Blade: Our History, Our Future.* New York: HarperCollins, 1987.

Favilli, Elena, and Francesca Cavallo. *Good Night Stories for Rebel Girls.* Los Angeles: Timbuktu Labs, 2017.

Frankl, Viktor. *Man's Search for Meaning.* Boston: Beacon Press, 2006.

Franklin, Benjamin. Quote at the US Constitution Center. https://constitutioncenter.org.

Goldberg, Natalie. *Writing Down the Bones: Freeing the Writer Within.* Boston: Shambhala Publications, 1986.

Hanh, Thich Nhat. *Peace Is Every Step: The Path of Mindfulness in Everyday Life*. New York: Bantam, 1992.

Humes, James C. *The Wit and Wisdom of Winston Churchill.* New York: Harper Perennial, 1995.

Jefferson, Thomas. Letter to William Duane. 1811. https://foundersquotes.com.

Kennedy, John F. Final Address to the United Nations General Assembly, September 20, 1963. New York.

King, Martin Luther, Jr. *Letter from the Birmingham Jail.* New York: HarperOne, 1994.

King, Martin Luther, Jr. Speech delivered at the Lincoln Memorial, August 28, 1963.

Lamott, Anne. *Grace (Eventually): Thoughts on Faith.* New York: Riverhead Books, 2008.

Largent, Christopher. *The Best Advice in History: Epictetus' Manual for Living.* North Charleston, SC: CreateSpace Independent Publishing, 2017.

Lepore, Jill. *These Truths: A History of the United States.* New York: W. W. Norton, 2018.

Lesser, Elizabeth. *Broken Open: How Difficult Times Can Help Us Grow.* New York: Villard Books, 2005.

Lincoln, Abraham. First Inaugural Address, March 4, 1861.

Lincoln, Abraham. House Divided Speech, June 16, 1858. Springfield, Illinois.

Massieu, Jean-Baptiste. *A Collection of the Most Remarkable Definitions and Answers of Massieu and Clerc.* Translated by J. H. Sievrac. London: Cox and Baylis, 1815.

Melville, Herman. *Moby Dick.* Scotts Valley, CA: CreateSpace Independent Publishing Platform, 2018.

Meyer, Danny. *Setting the Table: The Transforming Power of Hospitality in Business.* New York: Harper Collins, 2009.

Mitchell, Stephen. *Tao Te Ching: A New English Version.* New York: HarperCollins, 1991.

Morrison, Toni. *Beloved.* New York: Alfred A. Knopf Inc., 1987.

Nepo, Mark. *The Book of Awakening: Having the Life You Want by Being Present to the Life You Have.* Berkeley, CA: Conari Press, 2000.

Newman, John. "Amazing Grace," 1779.

Oliver, Mary. *Wild Geese.* Northumberland, UK: Bloodaxe Books, 2004.

Osbon, Diane K. *Reflections on the Art of Living: A Joseph Campbell Companion.* New York: HarperCollins, 1991.

Pope, Alexander. "An Essay on Criticism." 1711.

Ricard, Mattieu, and Trinh Thuan. *The Quantum and the Lotus: A Journey to the Frontiers Where Science and Buddhism Meet.* New York: Broadway Books, 2004.

Rilke, Rainer Maria. *Letters to a Young Poet.* New York: W. W. Norton, 1993.

Roosevelt, Eleanor. *You Learn by Living: Eleven Keys for a More Fulfilling Life.* Reprint edition. New York: Harper Perennial, 2016.

Rosling, Hans, with Ola Rosling and Anna Rosling Rönnlund. *Factfulness: Ten Reasons We're Wrong about the World—And Why Things Are Better Than You Think.* New York: Flatiron Books, 2018.

Rumi, Jalal al-Din. *The Essential Rumi.* Translated by Coleman Barks. New York: Harper One, 2004.

de Saint-Exupéry, Antoine. *The Little Prince.* Translated by Katherine Woods, London: Piccolo Books, 1974.

Seeley, Thomas D. *Honeybee Democracy.* Princeton, NJ: Princeton University Press, 2010.

Seligman, Martin E. P. *Flourish: A Visionary New Understanding of Happiness and Well-Being.* Reprint edition. New York: Atria Books, 2012.

Seppälä, Emma M., *https://emmaseppala.com/3-ways-social-media-ruins-everything*.

Sheldon, W. L. *What to Believe: An Ethical Creed.* Philadelphia: S. Burns Weston, 1894.

Sinek, Simon. *Start with Why: How Great Leaders Inspire Everyone to Take Action.* London: Portfolio, 2009.

Stanton, Elizabeth Cady, Susan B. Anthony, Matilda Joslyn Gage, and Ida Husted Harper. *History of Woman Suffrage. Volume 4.* New York: Fowler & Wells, 1902.

Steindl-Rast, David. *Want to Be happy? Be Grateful.* TED Talk. TEDGlobal, 2013.

Tennyson, Alfred. "Ulysses." *Poems.* London: Edward Moxon, 1842.

Thoreau, Henry David. *Walden.* Boston: Ticknor and Fields, 1854.

Twist, Lynne with Teresa Barker. *The Soul of Money: Reclaiming the Wealth of Our Inner Resources.* New York: W.W. Norton & Company, 2003.

Viscott, David S. *Finding Your Strength in Difficult Times: A Book of Meditations.* Chicago: Contemporary Books, 1993.

White. E. B. *Letters of Hope.* Compiled by Shaun Usher. San Francisco: Chronicle Books, 2014.

Winfrey, Oprah. "Oprah's Forgiveness Aha! Moment." Oprah's Life Class, Oprah Winfrey Network.

Yousafzai, Malala. *I Am Malala: The Story of the Girl Who Stood Up for Education and Was Shot by the Taliban.* Co-written with Christina Lamb. New York: Little, Brown and Company, 2013.